David Sutherland

A Tour up the Straits, from Gibraltar to Constantinople

With the Leading Events in the Present War Between the Austrians, Russians, and

Turks, to the Commencement of the Year 1789

David Sutherland

A Tour up the Straits, from Gibraltar to Constantinople
With the Leading Events in the Present War Between the Austrians, Russians, and Turks, to the Commencement of the Year 1789

ISBN/EAN: 9783337167011

Printed in Europe, USA, Canada, Australia, Japan

Cover: Foto ©Andreas Hilbeck / pixelio.de

More available books at **www.hansebooks.com**

A

TOUR UP THE STRAITS,

FROM

GIBRALTAR

TO

CONSTANTINOPLE.

WITH THE

LEADING EVENTS IN THE PRESENT WAR

BETWEEN THE

AUSTRIANS, RUSSIANS, AND THE TURKS,

TO THE

COMMENCEMENT OF THE YEAR 1789.

By CAPTAIN SUTHERLAND,

OF THE 25th REGIMENT.

LONDON:

PRINTED FOR THE AUTHOR;

AND SOLD BY J. JOHNSON, N° 72, ST. PAUL'S CHURCH-
YARD.

M.DCC.XC.

TO

THE RIGHT HONORABLE

LADY LOUISA LENNOX,

THIS VOLUME

IS

MOST RESPECTFULLY INSCRIBED,

BY HER LADYSHIP's

MOST OBLIGED,

MOST FAITHFUL, AND

MOST OBEDIENT SERVANT,

D. SUTHERLAND.

INTRODUCTION.

THE Commander in Chief of the garrison of Gibraltar having indulged the Author of the following pages with leave of absence, he accepted an invitation from an amiable Friend, to accompany him on a Voyage to the Levant.

It was with the most heart-felt satisfaction, that he found himself enabled to profit by so favorable an opportunity of visiting a country, not only

only interesting from the precious remains of antiquity with which it is still adorned, but from the critical state into which it was thrown by the war already began, which threatened, sooner or later, to involve in it many of the Powers of Europe, and to call forth the just arm of Great Britain, to check the haughty usurpations of the ambitious Court of Russia.

The Author's friends saw his happiness in embarking on such a Tour; and, that they might, in some degree, partake of it, one of them insisted that he should keep, and transmit him, a regular Journal.

This promise the Author readily gave, and faithfully observed.

INTRODUCTION.

The compliments paid to this little work, firſt gave him the idea of appearing in print. Aware, however, that the ground he had travelled over, had often been treated upon by much more able pens, he for ſome time ſuppreſſed his hopes of becoming a candidate for fame in the literary world: but, after the general encouragement he met, he would have been guilty of injuſtice to himſelf, and of want of confidence in his friends, had he any longer heſitated to appear before the Public.

LIST OF SUBSCRIBERS.

A.

Duchess Dowag. of Ancaster, *L.*
Duchess Dowag. of Athol
Countess Dowag. of Ailesbury
Earl of Aylesford, 5 *L.*
Earl of Abercorn
Right Hon. Lord Apsley, *L.*
Right Hon. Lady Apsley, *L.*
Le Chevalier Angelo
Miss F. Ashburnham, 2 Copies
Miss K. Ashburnham, 2 Copies
Mr. Aldridge, M. P. *L.*
Capt. Alms, Royal Navy, *L.*
Capt. Archer, 1st Reg. of Guards, *L.*
Capt. Airey, 48th Reg.
Lieut. Andrews, Royal Navy
Lieut. Aytone, 16th Reg.
Lieut. Adams, Queen's Reg.
Lieut. Anderson, 48th Reg.
Lieut. Archbald, 30th Reg.

Ensign Abbot, 68th Reg.
Ensign Alves, 35th Reg.
Mr. Adair, Pall-mall, *L.*
Mr. Adair, Newton, *L.*
Mr. Anderson, Gibraltar
Mr. Abudraham, Gibraltar
Mr. Ashton, Gibraltar
Mr. Acland, Devonshire
Mr. Arthur
Mr. Abney, St. John's College.

B.

Earl Bathurst, *L.*
Earl of Balcarres
Countess of Balcarres
Countess Dowag. of Balcarres
Right Hon. Lady Charlotte Bertie, *L.*
Right Hon. Isaac Barré, 5 *L.*
Lieut. General Sir Robert Boyd, K. B. *L.*
Hon. George Berkeley, *L.*
Hon. Mrs. Berkeley, *L.*
Sir Montague Burgoyne, Bart.
Sir Patrick Blake, Bart. *L.*
Hon. C. Boyle, Royal Navy
Mr. Barwell, M. P. 2 *L.*
Mrs. Barwell, *L.*
Mr. Brodie, M. P. *L.*
Mr. Bulteel, 3 *L.*
Mr. T. H. Bulteel, *L.*
Mr. J. Bulteel, Jun. *L.*
Colonel Bullock, M. P.
Governor Bruce, Dominica, 4 Copies

Governor Brown, Guernsey, L.
Colonel Balfour, 33d Reg.
Colonel Bromhead, R. N. Lincoln Militia
Colonel B. Bromhead, R. S. ditto
Major Brooke, 3d Dragoon Guards, L.
Capt. Bulteel, Royal Navy
Capt. Bennet, Royal Reg.
Capt. Baynes, Queen's Reg.
Capt. Booth, 32d Reg.
Capt. Braban, 38th Reg.
Capt. Richard Brine, L.
Capt. Robert Brine
Capt. Joseph Bourke
Capt. Brownrigg, 52d Reg.
Capt. Busby, 25th Reg. L.
Capt. Brown, Edinburgh
Mrs. Brown
Capt. Baynton, Queen's Reg.
Capt. Boardman, R. N. B. Dragoons
Capt. Bates, Inniskilling Dragoons
Capt. Brock, Guernsey
Capt. Baillie, 67th Reg.
Capt. Bain, ditto
Capt. Bromhead, R. N. Lincoln Militia
Capt. Bell, 19th Reg.
Capt. Berry
Rev. Dr. Blair, D. D.
Lieut. Brown, Royal Navy, 2 Copies
Lieut. Bowen, ditto
Lieut. Burlton, ditto
Lieut. Briggs, 25th Reg.
Lieut. Bunbury, 32d Reg.

Lieut. Brown, 35th Reg.
Lieut. Byng, 33d Reg.
Lieut. Browne, 19th Reg.
Lieut. Brock, 8th Reg.
Lieut. Bowes, 3d Reg.
Lieut. Bumford, 67th Reg.
Lieut. Bayne, 11th Reg. *L.*
Lieut. Bellamy, Essex Militia, *L.*
Lieut. Brooke, 48th Reg.
Lieut. Butler, 67th Reg.
Ensign Bickford, 25th Reg.
Ensign Ball, ditto
Ensign Buchanan, 32d Reg.
Ensign Baynes, ditto
Ensign Bower, 59th Reg.
Ensign Brown, ditto
Ensign Blunt, 3d Reg.
Ensign Blakeney, 17th Reg.
Ensign Barnett, 12th Reg.
Ensign Baillie, 30th Reg.
Ensign Bunbury, 60th Reg.
Mr. Broughton, Royal Navy
Mr. Browne, ditto
Mr. Bushell, ditto
Mr. Boyle, 42d Reg.
Mr. Bridges, Royal Navy, 2 Copies
Mr. Becher, ditto, 4 Copies
Rev. Mr. Barnes, Sussex
Rev. Mr. Barslow, Colchester
Mr. Baynes, Gibraltar, 6 Copies
Mr. Bruciano, ditto
Mr. Bolton, ditto

Mr. Bryant, ditto
Mr. Barton, Colchester
Mr. C. Baring, Exeter, *L.*
Mrs. P. Baker, Exmouth, *L.*
Mr. Bailey, Ordnance
Mr. Barnard, Jersey
Mr. Broadley, Yorkshire
Mrs. Bull, Chichester
Mr. Burnett, Malaga
Mr. Brock, Guernsey
Mr. J. Brock, ditto
Mr. Baird, of Newbeath
Mr. W. Busby, *L.*
Mr. Bannatine
Mr. Backwell, Chichester
Mr. Bowman, Ashgrove
Mr. Bedingfield, Bromley-Hall

C.

Her Royal Highness the Duchess of Cumberland, *L.*
Marquis of Clanricarde, *L.*
Marchioness of Clanricarde, *L.*
Right Hon. General Conway, *L.*
Lady Campbell
Mr. Cotsford, M. P. *L.*
Mr. Crickitt, M. P.
Mr. Chambers, 2 *L.*
Mr. Cummings, Inglefield Green, 8 Copies
Capt. Cromwell, Royal Navy, *L.*
Colonel Coates, 19th Reg.
Colonel Caldecot, R. N. Lincoln Militia, *L.*

Colonel Campbell, Royal Reg.
Major Cockran, ditto
Major Cook, *L*
Major Campbell, 48th Reg.
Capt. D. Campbell, Royal Reg.
Capt. Conolly, 18th Reg.
Capt. Carter, 32d Reg.
Capt. Coutts, Marines
Capt. Carlton, Royal Artillery
Capt. Craufurd, Queen's Dragoon Guards
Capt. Campbell, 19th Reg.
Capt. Church, 38th Reg.
Capt. Cuppage, Royal Artillery
Capt. Carter, Suffex Militia, *L.*
Lieut. Commerford, Royal Navy
Lieut. Campbell, ditto
Lieut. Craven
Lieut. Croker, 38th Reg.
Lieut. Clepham, 17th Reg.
Lieut. Carleton, 3d Dragoon Guards *L.*
Lieut. A. Campbell, Royal Reg.
Lieut. N. Campbell, ditto
Lieut. R. Campbell, ditto
Lieut. Caulfield, 11th Reg.
Lieut. Chamney, 25th Reg.
Lieut. Campbell, ditto
Lieut. Coleman, 32d Reg.
Lieut. Cornifh, Marines, *L.*
Lieut. Clarke, 35th Reg.
Lieut. Childers, 11th Dragoons
Enfign Cochran, Royal Reg.
Enfign Chambers, Queen's Reg.

Enfign

(xv)

Enſign Cockell, ditto
Enſign Clapham, 35th Reg.
Enſign Cunningham, 17th Reg.
Enſign Callander, 25th Reg.
Enſign Creighton, 19th Reg.
Enſign Copley, 30th Reg.
Enſign Clements, 59th Reg.
Mr. Cook, 25th Reg.
Mr. Cook, 60th Reg.
Dr. Calcagni, LL. D. Naples
Rev. Mr. Campbell, Jamaica
Mr. Crathorne, *L.*
Mr. Collins, Royal Navy
Mr. Collier, ditto
Mr. Coſby, ditto
Mr. R. B. Campbell, ditto
Mr. G. R. Collyer, ditto
Mr. Coutts, Banker, *L.*
Mr. Claneley, Malaga
Mr. Cole, ditto
Mr. Crooke, ditto
Mr. Caſtleman, Ordnance
Mr. Collier, Wenlock
Mr. Colt, of Seacliff
Mr. Caravallo, Gibraltar
Mr. Carey, Guernſey
Mr. Cholmondeley
Mr. Cathcatt, of Greenfield
Mr. Corſellis, Collector of Colcheſter
Mr. Correwont, Jamaica
Mr. Cowper, Gibraltar, 2 Copies
Mr. M. Cowper, ditto

Mr.

Mr. M. Cowper, Jun. ditto
Mr. Calcraft, ditto

D.

Right Hon. Lord Daer, *L.*
Hon. Mrs. Damer, 2 *L.*
Sir Thomas Dundas, Bart. *L.*
Sir George Douglas, Bart. *L.*
Colonel Dundas, 11th Dragoons
Colonel Dalrymple, Queen's Reg.
Colonel Dundas, Royal Reg.
Colonel Dansey, 33d Reg.
Colonel D'Aubant, Royal Engineers
Capt. Dewry, Royal Navy
Capt. Dumaresque, ditto
Capt. Douglas, 11th Reg.
Capt. Davies, 38th Reg.
Capt. Darby, 59th Reg.
Captain Dorset, R. M. Academy
Capt. De Ruvijnes, Royal Artillery
Capt. Dickson, Kelso
Lieut. Dunham, Royal Navy
Lieut. Dewell, Queen's Reg.
Lieut. Dawson, ditto, *L.*
Lieut. Dickens, Royal Engineers
Lieut. Dowse, ditto
Lieut. Dickson, 25th Reg. 2 Copies
Lieut. Dalton, 67th Reg.
Lieut. Davie, 75th Reg. *L.*
Lieut. Drozier, Royal Artillery
Ensign Duff, 35th Reg.
Cornet Dupies, Queen's Dragoon Guards

Mr. Davies, 3d Dragoon Guards, *L.*
Dr. Downman, M. D. Exeter, *L.*
Dr. Douglas, M. D. Kelso
Dr. Dickson, Antigua
Mr. Durell, King's Advocate, Jersey
Rev. H. Bate Dudley
Mr. Drill, Royal Navy
Mr. Dowling, ditto
Mrs. Dewar, Edinburgh
Mrs. Disney, Lincoln, *L.*
Miss Anne Dick, Prestonfield
Mr. Ducarel, Exmouth, *L.*
Mr. Duff, Cadiz, 6 Copies
Mr. Dezé, Gibraltar
Mr. Dott, *L.*
Mr. Dunbar, Edinburgh
Mr. Day, Colchester
Mr. De Zea, Malaga
Mr. Desdive, ditto
Mr. Derrieux, ditto
Mr. Dannexy, ditto
Mr. Dempster
Mr. Dawson, Pontefract, *L.*
Mr. Dashwood
Mr. J. Drew, Chichester, 2 Copies
Mr. Dundas, of Arniston
Mr. Dundas, Lincoln's-Inn
Mr. Dundas, of Melville
Mr. Davies, Coombe Grove, *L.*
Mr. Ditcher, East Berghott
Mr. Donaldson, Jamaica

E.

Earl of Eglintoun, *L.*
Hon. Colonel Eliott, 3 Copies
Colonel Eyre, Royal Artillery
Major Edgar, 25th Reg. 8 Copies
Capt. Evelegh, Royal Engineers
Capt. Erskine, 50th Reg.
Lieut. Espinasse, 11th Reg.
Lieut. Eiston, 35th Reg.
Lieut. Elliott, King's Dragoon Guards
Lieut. Edwards, Queen's Reg.
Lieut. Evelegh, ditto
Lieut. Evatt, Queen's Dragoon Guards
Ensign Eyre, 11th Reg.
Ensign Elliot, 25th Reg. 2 Copies
Ensign Eliott, Queen's Reg.
Mr. Ekins, Royal Navy, 2 Copies
Mr. Elkins, ditto
Mrs. Elliot, Malaga
Mr. Enslie, Smyrna, 2 Copies
Mr. Eyre, Exmouth
Mr. Eden, Gibraltar
Mr. Elliot, Essex

F.

Right Hon. Lord Augustus Fitzroy
Right Hon. Lord Charles Fitzgerald, *L.*
Right Hon. Lord Henry Fitzgerald, *L.*
Right Hon. Lord Robert Fitzgerald, *L.*
Right Hon. Lord Edward Fitzgerald, *L.*
Hon. Colonel Fox, *L.*
Hon. Mrs. Fox
Hon. Mrs. Forward, *L.*

Hon. Matthew Fortescue, *L.*
Mr. Francis, M. P. *L.*
Mrs. Francis, *L.*
Miss Francis, *L.*
Miss C. Francis, *L.*
Colonel Fullarton, M. P. *L.*
Mr. Fleming, M. P. *L.*
Capt. Forch, Queen's Reg.
Capt. Fyers, Royal Engineers
Capt. Fiott, Jersey
Lieut. French, 35th Reg.
Lieut. Finley, Royal Engineers, 2 Copies
Lieut. Findlay, King's Dragoon Guards
Lieut. Freeman, Royal N. B. Dragoons
Lieut. Fellowes, 61st Reg.
Lieut. Farquharson, 42d Reg.
Lieut. Finney, Royal Reg.
Lieut. Framingham, Royal Artillery
Ensign Fitzgerald, 11th Reg.
Dr. Fleming, 25th Reg.
Mr. Fleming, ditto
Dr. Fellowes, M. D. Lincoln, *L.*
Rev. Dr. Foster, D. D. Colchester
Rev. Mr. Frewen, ditto
Professor Ferguson
Mr. Judge Fraser, Gibraltar, 2 Copies
Mr. Fraser, King's Arm's-Yard, 2 Copies
Mr. S. Fraser, Jun. ditto, 2 Copies
Mr. Finley, Royal Navy
Mr. Fraser, ditto
Mr. Franklin, ditto, 2 Copies
Mr. Farlier, ditto
Mrs. Frankland, Chichester, *L.*

Mrs. Fletcher, Edinburgh
Mrs. Fordyce, of Ayton
Miss Fergusson, St. Alban's
Mrs. Forbes, of Callander
Mr. Forbes
Mr. R. Forbes
Mr. Falconer, *L.*
Mr. Flor, Malaga
Mr. Ferguson, Pitfour

G.

Duchess of Gordon, *L.*
Earl Gower, *L.*
Right Hon. Lord Garlies, 2 Copies
Right Hon. Lord Adam Gordon
Hon. Mrs. Gawler, *L.*
Mr. Bellenden Gawler, *L.*
Mr. Gawler, Lincoln's Inn, *L.*
Major Gray, Queen's Reg.
Major Glover, 11th Reg.
Capt. Gordon, 16th Reg.
Capt. Giles, 19th Reg.
Capt. Gledstanes, 55th Reg.
Capt. Gardiner, 25th Reg. 4 Copies
Capt. Glynn, of Bodmin, *L.*
Mrs. Glynn, *L.*
Mr. Glynn, *L.*
Lieut. Graves, Royal Navy
Lieut. Gordon, Queen's Reg.
Lieut. Groves, ditto
Lieut. Garside, 59th Reg.
Lieut. Gore, 33d Reg.

Lieut. Gibson, Essex Militia
Lieut. Adam Gordon, 67th Reg.
Lieut. J. Gordon, ditto
Lieut. Gem, 19th Reg.
Lieut. Grant, ditto
Lieut. W. Grant, 55th Reg.
Cornet Graham, 3d Dragoon Guards, *L.*
Ensign Gayer, 67th Reg.
Ensign Godfrey, 32d Reg.
Dr. Graham, M. D. Royal Reg.
Mr. Groves, 67th Reg.
Mr. Griffiths, Turnham Green, *L.*
Mr. Godfrey, *L.*
Miss Godfrey, *L.*
Mr. Goring, *L.*
Mr. Gascoyne, *L.*
Mr. Goodenough, Tax Office, *L.*
Mr. Goddard, Royal Navy
Mr. Goate, ditto
Mr. Green, ditto
Rev. Mr. Green, Colchester
Rev. Mr. Graves, Claverton
Rev. Mr. Guy, Chichester
Mr. Guy, ditto
Mr. W. Guy, ditto
Mrs. Greenwood, Winchester
Mr. Gregory, Consul at Malaga
Mr. Gretten, Colchester
Mr. Grana, Malaga
Mr. Grey, Alicant
Mr. Griffiths, Chichester.

H.

Earl of Hopetoun, *L.*
Right Hon. Lord Herbert, *L.*
Right Hon. Lady Louisa Harvey, *L.*
Mr. Harvey, *L.*
Right Hon. W. Gerard Hamilton, *L.*
Hon. General Harcourt, *L.*
Hon. Mrs. Harcourt, *L.*
Sir William Hamilton, K. B. 3 Copies
Sir Henry Houghton, Bart. *L.*
Hon. Charles Hope, *L.*
Hon. John Hope, *L.*
Hon. Alexander Hope, *L.*
Mr. Hope
Hon. Mrs. Hunter
Colonel Home, Royal N. B. Dragoons
Major Hart, Inniskilling Dragoons
Major Hamilton, 18th Reg.
Major Haynes, 59th Reg.
Major Haynes, Winchester
Capt. Hertzog, 17th Reg.
Capt. Hewgill, Coldstream
Capt. Hawley, King's Dragoon Guards
Capt. Harrison, Essex Militia
Capt. Horne, 48th Reg.
Capt. Hely, 11th Reg.
Capt. Haig, 35th Reg.
Capt. Howorth, Royal Artillery, *L.*
Capt. Hayes, 11th Dragoons
Lieut. Hext, 22d Reg.
Lieut. Hall, King's Dragoon Guards
Lieut. Hall, 30th Reg.

Lieut.

Lieut. Hutton, Royal Artillery
Lieut. Hamilton, ditto
Lieut. Hooke, ditto
Lieut. Hope, 18th Reg.
Lieut. Hewan, 25th Reg.
Lieut. Haven, 50th Reg.
Lieut. Hill, 68th Reg.
Lieut. Hamilton, ditto
Lieut. Harnage, 11th Dragoons
Enfign Hucks, 22d Reg. *L.*
Enfign Hinde, 25th Reg.
Enfign Hawes, 59th Reg.
Enfign Hinuber, 68th Reg.
Cornet Hunter, King's Dragoon Guards
Cornet Hamilton, Royal N. B. Dragoons
Enfign Hinde, 55th Reg.
Enfign Horsford, 67th Reg.
Enfign Hartley, ditto
Mr. Hamilton, Queen's Dragoon Guards
Mr. Hudfon, Commiffioner at Gibraltar
Mrs. Hudfon
Mr. Harris, Royal Navy
Mr. Hughes, ditto
Mr. Horton, ditto, 4 Copies
Mr. Halliday, ditto
Rev. Mr. Harrifon, Effex
Rev. Mr. Hewitt, Colchefter
Dr. Heriot, M. D. Jerfey
Mr. Horne, Writer to the Signet
Mrs. Holt, Chefter
Mrs. Home, Winchefter
Mrs. Heathfield, Chichefter

Mrs. Hay, of Mountblainy
Mr. Heathfield, of Nutwell, *L.*
Mr. A. Heathfield
Mr. Horsey, Gibraltar
Mr. Hamilton, of Wishaw, *L.*
Mr. Harcourt, Edinburgh
Mr. Hume, ditto
Mr. D. Hamilton, ditto
Mr. Hadley, Essex, *L.*
Mr. Hodson, Malaga
Mr. Huclin, ditto
Mr. Hoffman, ditto
Mr. Hounsom, Funtington
Mr. Henchman, Chester
Mr. Hamilton, of Grange
Mr. Hamilton, of Pencaitland
Mr. Heigelin, Naples
Mr. Hayley, Chichester
Mr. Heming, ditto
Mr. G. Heming, ditto
Mr. Hatcher, Gosport
Mr. Havens, Colchester
Mr. R. Havens, ditto
Mr. Hassard, ditto

J.

Colonel Johnston, 17th Reg.
Colonel Jones
Major Jordain, *L.*
Capt. Johnston, 59th Reg. *L.*
Capt. Jones, Queen's Reg.
Capt. Imrie, Royal Reg.

Lieut.

Lieut. Johnston, 17th Reg.
Ensign Ironside, 68th Reg.
Cornet Johnston, Inniskilling Dragoons
Ensign Jardine, 12th Reg.
Rev. Mr. T. Jarvis, Devon
Rev. Mr. J. Jarvis, ditto
Mr. Jackson, *L.*
Mr. P. Justice, Drayton, *L.*
Mr. Jeffrays
Mr. W. Johnston, Chichester.

K.

Major Kay, 12th Reg. *L.*
Lieut. Kelly, 32d Reg.
Lieut. Karr, ditto
Lieut. Kelly, 68th Reg.
Lieut. Kersteman, Royal Engineers
Lieut. Kingsbury, Essex Militia
Lieut. R. Kingsbury, ditto
Lieut. Knight, 11th Reg.
Ensign Kingsberry, Queen's Reg.
Ensign Kerr, 48th Reg.
Rev. Mr. Keun, Smyrna
Miss Keppel, *L.*
Miss Anne Keith
Miss Kinloch
Mr. Kinloch
Mr. A. Kinloch
Mr. Keck, Wimpole-street, *L.*
Mrs. Keck, *L.*
Mr. Kenworthy, *L.*
Mr. Keeting, *L.*

Mr. Kearney, *L.*
Mr. Kerfteman, Colchefter
Mr. King, ditto
Mr. Kirpatrick, Malaga

L.

Literary Society at Lincoln, *L.*
Duke of Leinfter, *L.*
Right Hon. Lord George Lennox, 3 *L.*
Right Hon. Lady Louifa Lennox, 3 *L.*
Right Hon. Lady Charlotte Lenox, *L.*
Colonel Lenox, *L.*
Hon. General Leflie, *L.*
Hon. David Leflie
Hon. Robert Lindfey
Hon. Mrs. Lindfey
Commodore Lutwidge
Mr. Richard Lee, Smyrna, 10 Copies
Mr. Edward Lee, ditto, 10 Copies
Capt. Lane, 32d Reg.
Capt. Lawfon, Royal Artillery
Lieut. Lane, King's Dragoon Guards
Lieut. Lifter, ditto
Lieut. Lynn, Marines
Lieut. Lumfden, 55th Reg.
Lieut. Lyne, 19th Reg.
Mr. Lavie, Royal Navy
Enfign Lewin, 50th Reg.
Enfign Lowe, ditto
Enfign Lucas, 68th Reg.
Cornet Lyons, 11th Dragoons
Cornet Lambe, King's Light Dragoons

Cornet

Cornet Le Marchant, Inniskilling Dragoons
Ensign Lloyd, 11th Reg.
Dr. Lend, 19th Reg.
Mr. Lee, 17th Reg.
Mr. H. Lynne, Royal Navy
Mr. Lamborn, ditto, 4 Copies
Mr. Lawrence, ditto, 2 Copies
Mr. Lee, Lymston, L.
Rev. Mr. Lee
Mrs. Lindegrene, Portsmouth
Mr. Lovelace, Malaga, 2 Copies
Mr. Lovejoy, ditto
Mr. Lagassicke, Devon
Mr. Lewis
Mr. Lewis, A. B. Colchester
Mr. Lys, Gosport

M.

Duke of Marlborough, L.
Earl of Mount Edgcumbe, L.
Viscount Mountstuart, L.
Sir William Maxwell, Bart.
Sir John Macpherson, Bart.
Sir John Maxwell, Bart.
Hon. George H. Monson, L.
Hon. Miss Mackay
Hon. Miss Georgina Mackay
Mrs. Meynell, L.
Mrs. Milbanke, L.
General Martin
Colonel Maister, M. P. L.
Mr. Morier, Smyrna, 10 Copies

Mr. Maltafs, Smyrna, 5 Copies
Colonel Maxwell, 30th Reg.
Colonel Morris, Invalids
Colonel Mercer, Royal Engineers, L.
Capt. Mann, Royal Navy
Capt. G. Murray, ditto
Major Mawby, 18th Reg.
Capt. Manley, Royal Artillery
Capt. Montagu, Queen's Reg.
Capt. Moncrief, 11th Reg.
Capt. Montrefor, 18th Reg.
Capt. Macartney, 32d Reg.
Capt. M'Leod, 59th Reg.
Capt. M'Lean, 68th Reg.
Capt. Mitchell, 11th Dragoons
Capt. Maitland, 1ft Reg. of Guards
Capt. Mackewan, 38th Reg.
Capt. Martin, 12th Reg.
Capt. Macleod, Royal Artillery, L.
Capt. Marriott, Effex Militia
Capt. Martin, 60th Reg.
Capt. Marfhall, 30th Reg.
Capt. M'Cullock, ditto
Captain M'Murdo, 3d Reg.
Capt. Money, Royal N. Lincoln Militia
Lieut. Molineux, 25th Reg. L.
Lieut. Mackenzie, Royal Reg.
Lieut. Maitland, Queen's Reg.
Lieut. Maddifon, 22d Reg.
Lieut. Maclean, 50th Reg.
Lieut. Moneypenny, 68th Reg.
Lieut. Mytton, 25th Reg.

Lieut. Marriott, Essex Militia
Lieut. Maxwell, 48th Reg.
Lieut. Montgomery, 3d Reg.
Ensign Macdonald, Royal Reg.
Ensign M'Kellar, ditto
Ensign Maxwell, 18th Reg.
Cornet Mackenzie, 11th Dragoons
Cornet Mathew, Royal Dragoons
Ensign Marton, 22d Reg.
Ensign Montgomery, 30th Reg.
Ensign Macdonald, 19th Reg.
Ensign M'Donell, 3d Reg.
Mr. M'Donald, 11th Reg.
Mrs. Maitland, Edinburgh
Mrs. Martin, Portsmouth
Mrs. Munn, Greenwich, L.
Mrs. Mitchell, Jersey
Miss M'Adam, of Graigingillan
Mr. Maule, Royal Navy
Mr. Mitchell, ditto
Dr. M'Donald, M. D. Antigua
Rev. Mr. Macklin, Essex
Mr. Moir, Writer to the Signet
Mr. Morrison, Gibraltar, 2 Copies
Mr. Meyrick, Queen's Reg.
Mr. Macdonald, Edinburgh
Mr. Moneypenny, ditto
Mr. Manning
Mr. G. H. Morisner
Mr. Murphy, Malaga
Mr. J. S. Macnamara, ditto
Mr. T. Macnamara, ditto

Mr. Mackintosh, Bathford, *L.*
Mr. Mackintosh, John-street, *L.*
Mr. Marchetti, Naples
Mr. M'Kinnon, ditto
Mr. Mackay, *L.*
Mr. M'Adam, of Dunaskire
Mr. Martin, Antigua
Mr. Massie, St. John's College

N.

Duke of Northumberland, *L.*
Capt. Newland, Chichester
Capt. Nichols
Lieut. Need, King's Dragoon Guards
Mrs. Newte, Exmouth, *L.*
Rev. Mr. Nott, *L.*
Mr. Newman, Malaga
Mr. R. Newland, Chichester
Mr. J. Newland, ditto
Mr. Neven, Gibraltar
Mr. Noble, Naples

O.

Earl of Orford, 2 *L.*
General O'Hara, 4 Copies
Sir William Oglander, Bart. *L.*
Rev. Dr. Oglander, *L.*
Rev. Mr. Oglander, *L.*
Mr. Oglander, *L.*
Capt. O'Hara, Royal Navy
Capt. O'Meara, 68th Reg.
Capt. Oakes, 33d Reg.

(xxxi)

Capt. Otway, 48th Reg.
Lieut. Ogilvie, 50th Reg.
Enfign Overend, ditto
Mr. Ofborne, Royal Navy
Mr. Ormfton, Kelfo

P.

Right Hon. Lord Paget, *L.*
Right Hon. Lady Caroline Peachey, *L.*
Right Hon. William Pitt, *L.*
Right Hon. Thomas Pelham, *L.*
Hon. William Paget, 2 Copies
General Phillipfon, *L.*
General Picton, *L.*
Admiral Peyton
Commiffioner Proby, *L.*
Colonel Phipps, Royal Engineers, 6 Copies
Mr. Phipps, Somerfet-ftreet, *L.*
Colonel Pringle, Royal Engineers
Capt. Peyton, Royal Navy, 2 Copies
Major Polfon, *L.*
Mr. Polfon, *L.*
Major Pitcairn, 17th Reg.
Capt. Prevoft, 25th Reg. 4 Copies
Capt. Peter, 23d Reg.
Lieut. Probyn, 38th Reg. *L.*
Lieut. Phipps, Royal Engineers, *L.*
Lieut. Picton, 12th Reg.
Lieut. Pell, 11th Reg. *L.*
Lieut. Powell, 18th Reg.
Lieut. Prevoft, 60th Reg.
Lieut. Petrie, 3d Reg.

Lieut.

Lieut. Prevoſt, ditto
Enſign Philpot, Queen's Reg.
Enſign Peep
Rev. Dr. Pennington, D. D.
Mrs. Pennington
Rev. Mr. Phillips, Devonſhire
Mr. Peachey, Binderton
Mrs. Peachey
Miſs Pulteney
Miſs Polluck, Lincoln
Mrs. E. Pownoll, Drayton, L.
Mrs. Peckham, Chicheſter
Mr. Partridge, Royal Navy
Mr. Phipps, ditto
Mr. Peters, ditto
Mr. Palmer, ditto
Mr. Pulk, L.
Mr. Perring, L.
Mr. Proby, Inner Temple
Mr. Piele, Harcourt Buildings
Mr. Plowes, Malaga, 2 Copies
Mr. M. Power, ditto
Mr. J. Power, ditto
Mr. Plunket, ditto

Q.

Lieut. Quin, 35th Reg.
Mr. T. Quilty, Malaga
Mr. J. Quilty, ditto

R.

Duke of Richmond, 2 L.
Duchess of Richmond, L. 5 Copies
Right Hon. Lady Reay
Sir Thomas Rumbold, Bart. 2 L.
Lady Rumbold, L.
Lady Rivers
Hon. Philip Roper, L.
Mrs. Rigby, Roefield, 2 L.
Colonel F. Hale Rigby, Essex Militia
Capt. Riddell, 32d Reg. 4 Copies
Capt. Raitt, Queen's Reg.
Capt. Richardson, 18th Reg.
Capt. Rose, 50th Reg.
Capt. James Robb, L.
Lieut. Rudsdell, 11th Reg.
Lieut. Ramsay, Queen's Reg.
Lieut. Rainy, 18th Reg.
Lieut. Ross, 25th Reg.
Lieut. Rowley, 68th Reg.
Lieut. Reeves, Royal Reg. L.
Lieut. Rowley, Royal Engineers
Ensign Robertson, Royal Reg.
Ensign Raleigh, Queen's Reg.
Ensign Raleigh, 11th Reg.
Ensign Robertson, 32d Reg.
Ensign Richardson, 35th Reg.
Ensign Rogers, 3d Reg.
Mr. Russell, 30th Reg.
Mr. Robinson, Adjutant of Gibraltar
Mr. Rhodes, King's Dragoon Guards
Rev. Mr. Rouse, T.

Mr. Raleigh, Gibraltar
Mr. Rofs, *L.*
Mr. Ramus, *L.*
Mr. Rofs, Gibraltar
Mr. A. Rofs, Ordnance, Gibraltar
Mr. A. Rofs, Gibraltar
Mrs. Rebow, Colchester
Mrs. Ruth, ditto
Mr. Round, ditto
Mr. Reynolds, Effex
Mr. Round, ditto
Mr. Rufh, Colchester
Mr. Rofden
Mr. W. Raper, Chichefter

S.

Countefs of Sutherland, *L.*
Right Hon. Lady Saltoun, 2 Copies
Right Hon. Lord Southampton, *L.*
Right Hon. Lady Madelina Sinclair, *L.*
Sir Robert Sinclair, Bart. *L.*
Lady Sinclair
Mifs Sinclair, *L.*
Dr. Sinclair, M. D.
Mr. Sinclair
Hon. Capt. Stopford, Royal Navy
Hon. G. A. Chetwynd Stapylton, *L.*
Hon. Mrs. Chetwynd Stapylton, *L.*
Mrs. Stapylton, *L.*
Hon. Cornet Southwell, *L.*
Mr. Steele, M. P. 2 *L.*
Mr. Steele, Recorder of Chichefter, *L.*

Mrs.

Mrs. Steele, Chichester, *L.*
Mr. Scottney, *L.*
Mr. Sargent, Lavington, *L.*
Mrs. Sargent, *L.*
Capt. Sutherland, Royal Navy, 2 Copies
Capt. Smith, ditto
Major Schaw, 68th Reg.
Major Strutt, 60th Reg.
Major Sladden, 67th Reg.
Capt. Snowe, 64th Reg.
Capt. John Smith, Royal Artillery
Capt. Scott, Royal Reg.
Capt. St. Clair, 25th Reg. 2 Copies
Capt. Shaw, 35th Reg.
Capt. Smith, Invalids
Capt. Smith, 25th Reg. 2 *L.*
Capt. Smith, Marlborough-street, *L.*
Capt. Skinner, Royal Engineers, *L.*
Capt. Scott, of Rosebank
Capt. Semple, 44th Reg. *L.*
Capt. Sperling, Essex Militia
Capt. Shipley, Royal Engineers
Capt. Sherret, 19th Reg.
Capt. Syer, King's Dragoon Guards
Lieut. J. Skinner, Royal Navy
Lieut. Stratton, ditto
Lieut. Sheldrake, Royal Artillery
Lieut. Skyring, ditto
Lieut. Shrapnell, ditto
Lieut. Sebright, 18th Reg.
Lieut. Scott, 32d Reg.
Lieut. Stewart, 25th Reg. 2 Copies

Lieut. Sturgeon, Marines
Lieut. Smart, Royal Engineers
Lieut. Serjeantſon, King's Dragoon Guards
Lieut. Saumarez, 8th Reg.
Lieut. Stratton, 67th Reg.
Lieut. Smith, 30th Reg.
Lieut. Sparrow, Eſſex Militia
Enſign St. George, 11th Reg.
Cornet Shelly, 11th Dragoons
Enſign Shirley, 67th Reg.
Enſign Sinclair, 3d Reg.
Mr. Shapter, Royal N. B. Dragoons
Mr. Smith, Denbigh Militia
Rev. Mr. Shillilo, Colcheſter
Rev. Mr. Sandys, Eſſex
Mr. Smith, Ordnance, *L.*
Mr. Snipe, Royal Navy
Mr. Scott, ditto
Mr. Simpſon, ditto
Mr. Smith, ditto
Mr. J. W. Skinner, ditto
Mr. Sneyd, ditto
Mr. Starck, ditto, 4 Copies
Mr. Scrivener, *L.*
Mr. Stables, *L.*
Mr. Storey, *L.*
Mr. Saumarez, Guernſey
Mrs. Sperling, Colcheſter
Mr. Simpſon, Ruſſian Conſul at Gibraltar
Mr. A. Simpſon, Gibraltar, *L.*
Mr. Smith, ditto
Mr. Stones, ditto

Mr.

Mr. Sweatland, ditto
Mr. W. Simpson, ditto
Mr. Smith, Bury St. Edmunds

T.

Sir George Thomas, Bart. *L.*
Mr. Tierney, M. P. *L.*
Miss E. S. Tayler, *L.*
Colonel Teasdale, *L.*
Major Trench, 38th Reg.
Capt. Timms, 44th Reg. *L.*
Capt. Tweedie, 12th Reg.
Capt. Trotter, King's Dragoon Guards
Capt. J. Thompson
Capt. J. Tiddy
Lieut. Tireman, Royal Navy
Lieut. Teesdale, 25th Reg. 2 Copies
Lieut. Turner, 3d Dragoon Guards, *L.*
Lieut. Thorley, 44th Reg.
Lieut. Tyndale, King's Dragoon Guards
Ensign Tomlinson, 30th Reg.
Cornet Thomas, 11th Dragoons
Mr. Taylor, 32d Reg.
Mr. Taylor, 67th Reg.
Mr. Thompson, 30th Reg.
Rev. Mr. Tireman, Chichester, 2 Copies
Rev. Cook Tylden
Mr. Teppet, Royal Navy
Mr. J. G. Thompson, ditto
Mr. Trownsell, ditto
Mr. R. Thompson, ditto
Mr. Tait, Edinburgh

Mr. Travers, *L.*
Mr. Tylburn, Colchester
Mr. Tabor, ditto
Mr. Tyssen, Essex
Mr. Tylden
Mr. Tinling, Gosport
Mr. Tobin, Malaga, 4 Copies

U.

Earl of Uxbridge, 2 *L.*
Countess of Uxbridge, *L.*
Capt. Urquhart, 30th Reg.
Mr. Upsman, Royal Navy
Mr. C. Upham, Exeter.

V.

Colonel Vyse, King's Dragoon Guards
Lieut. Vesey, 11th Reg.
Lieut. Vassell, 59th Reg.
Lieut. Vaughan, ditto, *L.*
Lieut. Vansittart, 38th Reg.
Lieut. Vincent, 19th Reg.
Dr. Veitch, Clithero, *L.*
Mr. Vaughan
Mr. Vaughan, Gibraltar

W.

Earl of Winchelsea, 2 *L.*
Viscountess Wicklow, *L.*
Sir John Wrottesly, Bart.
Sir James Wemyss, Bart.
Hon. Mr. Walpole, *L.*

Mr. Watson, of New Saughton, *L.*
Mr. Wallace, of Carlton Hall, *L.*
Colonel Walker, Royal Artillery
Major Wilson, Colchester, 2 Copies
Major Wauchope, 50th Reg.
Capt. Warre, Royal Navy
Capt. Williamson, 25th Reg. 4 Copies
Capt. Wright, ditto, 4 Copies
Capt. Wilson, 59th Reg.
Capt. Wilkinson, 67th Reg.
Lieut. Wade, 25th Reg. 2 Copies
Lieut. White, 32d Reg.
Lieut. Wilson, 50th Reg.
Lieut. Waugh, 68th Reg.
Lieut. Westroppe, Marines
Lieut. Wilson, 48th Reg.
Lieut. Willimot, 3d Reg.
Lieut. Wigley, Royal N. B. Dragoons
Cornet Webb, Queen's Dragoon Guards
Ensign Wolseley, 18th Reg.
Ensign Wogan, 12th Reg.
Dr. Walker, Edinburgh
Dr. Watson, Kelso
Mrs. Webber, Chichester, *L.*
Mrs. Willis
Mr. H. R. Williams, Royal Navy, 4 Copies
Mr. C. Williams, ditto, 2 Copies
Mr. Wright, Royal Navy
Mr. Wilson, ditto
Mr. Walker, ditto
Mr. Watts, ditto
Mr. Williams, *L.*

Mr. Welch, *L.*
Mr. White, 3 Copies
Mr. Williamson, *L.*
Mr. J. Williams, Exeter, *L.*
Mr. H. Woodfall, Cadiz
Mr. Winter, Gibraltar
Mr. Williams, ditto
Mr. Whitfield, Wenlock
Mr. Wood, Chichester
Mr. W. Sinclair Wemyss
Mr. Wistrer, Colchester
Mr. Walsond, Dominica
Mr. Worseley, Malaga
Mr. Wilson, Pontefract

Y.

Right Hon. Lady Elizabeth Yorke
Hon. Philip Yorke
Colonel Yorke, 33d Reg.
Capt. Yorke, Royal Artillery
Lieut. Young, Royal Navy, 4 Copies
Mr. Young, ditto
Mr. Yorston, Gibraltar.

☞ The Subscribers marked *L.* subscribed to the Guinea Edition, which the Author had not determined to publish till after he had collected the subscriptions at Gibraltar.

CONTENTS.

LETTER I.

Page

CEUTA—Goths and Saracens—Almeria—Rocks of Abibo - - - -   1

LETTER II.

Carthagena—War of the Succession - 12

LETTER III.

Reception at Cagliari—Lucilla - - 24

LETTER

LETTER IV.

Churches—Ball at the Palace—Trade, &c. of Sardinia - - - - - - 37

LETTER V.

Island of Capria—Tiberius—Malonia - 46

LETTER VI.

Excursion to Baia - - - - - - 49

LETTER VII.

Mount Vesuvius—The Hermit—Bay of Naples - - - - - - - - - 64

LETTER VIII.

Capo de Monte—Portici—Herculaneum—Pompeia - - - - - - - - 75

LETTER IX.

Casertta—St. Januarius—Opera—Government - - - - - - - - 86

LETTER X.

Visit to the King of Naples at Castello Mare—The Queen—Coast of Salerno—Pestum - - - - - - - - - 97

LETTER XI.

Lipari Islands—Volcano of Strombolo - 106

LETTER XII.

Messina—Earthquake—Scylla and Charybdis—Sir George Byng—Commodore Walton - - - - - - - - 112

LETTER XIII.

A fireball—Zante—Ithaca—Promontory of Leucate—Turks and Greeks - - 124

LETTER XIV.

Pirates—Milo—Paros—Attica—Sunium 139

LETTER XV.

Smyrna—Great Advantages to be derived from the Turkey Trade—Necessity of a regular Lazaretto in England - 158

LETTER XVI.

Cause of the War—The Russian Minister is sent to the Seven Towers—Turkish Manifesto—Attempt on Kimbourn—A Russian Ship of sixty-four guns gives herself up to the Turks—Ambitious Views of the two Imperial Courts—The Interest of England greatly endangered by them—Necessity of our opposing the Empress - - - - - - - 169

LETTER XVII.

Journey to Ephesus—The poor Girl—Caravansera—Temple of Diana—Character of the Turkish Ministers—The Vice-Admiral of the Porte beheaded - - - - - - - 189

LETTER XVIII.

Scyros—Idra—History of Athens - - 209

LETTER XIX.

Present State of Athens—Battle of Marathon - - - - - - - - - 225

LETTER XX.

Greek and Mahometan Religion - - 241

LETTER XXI.

Voyage from Athens to Leghorn - - 258

LETTER XXII.

Journey from Leghorn to Florence—Government of Peter Leopold—Public Ornaments—Palaces, Ricardi and Gerrini - - - - - - - - - 263

LETTER XXIII.

Gallery of Florence - - - - - - 275

CONTENTS.

LETTER XXIV.

Island of Elba—Mount Vesuvius - - 292

LETTER XXV.

Voyage to Palermo—Grotesque Statues—Funeral of Prince Palagonia - - 297

LETTER XXVI.

Attempt upon Belgrade—The Emperor declares War—Operations in Croatia—Prince Lichtenstein defeated by the Turks—The Emperor takes the Field in Person—The Prince of Moldavia deserts from the Turks - - - - - - 307

LETTER XXVII.

The Prince of Saxe Cobourg invests Choczim—Siege of Oczakow—Marshal Laudohn—Political Observations—Meadia taken by the Turks—The Grand Vizir defeats the Emperor - - - 325

LETTER XXVIII.

Passage through the Dardanelles—Constantinople - - - - - - - 346

LETTER XXIX.

Conclusion of the Campaign 1788 - - 360

Advertisement - - - - - - - 369

A TOUR FROM GIBRALTAR TO CONSTANTINOPLE.

LETTER I.

TO CAPTAIN SMITH.

Carthagena, August 14th.

MY DEAR FRIEND,

IN compliance with your request, I I have kept a regular Journal of my Voyage, which I now inclose you:

Tuesday, August 7th, Noon.

At eight o'clock, yesterday morning, we left Gibraltar, with a contrary wind; and, on the first tack, we passed Ceuta, a place of no great intrinsic value, and but an indifferent port. It is situated on a peninsula of Africa, which, with Gibraltar, Spartel and Traflagar, forms the Straits, and is so strongly fortified by Nature, that, although the Moors have often besieged it, it has withstood all their efforts.

Count Julian was Governor of this place, at the time Roderigo ravished his daughter, the beautiful *Cava*. The Count, inflamed with rage at the dishonor perpetrated on his family, and distracted at the ruin of his own child, forgot his duty to his country, which no private injuries can excuse, and engaged to put the Moors in possession of Spain, if they would revenge him on his abandoned Monarch.

It is not easy to determine who were the first inhabitants of Spain. We know that it was subdued by the Carthaginians before the Christian æra, and that they were

were conquered by the Romans; who, in their turn, yielded to the Goths, from whom Roderigo was descended.

At this time, the Saracens (the name the followers of Mahomet assumed) emigrating from Arabia, had overrun the neighbouring parts of Africa, which they have kept possession of ever since. To these people, Count Julian, with great truth, represented Roderic as a Prince universally detested, and whose tyranny promised a general insurrection among the Goths. The Saracen Chief at first doubted the Count's sincerity, but at last sent over a large army, which gained a complete victory over Roderigo, who was killed in the action; and the whole country submitted to the Moors.

A.D. 712.

Divisions arising among the conquerors, the natives, in less than six years, again appeared in arms, and the Saracens gradually

dually declined for near two centuries. Almanzor then arofe, and, by his repeated victories, revived the affairs of his countrymen: But, on the death of this great General, the Chriftians again made head, and reduced the Moors to fuch ftraits, that, although Mahomet Ben Jofeph, Sovereign of Barbary, came over to their affiftance with all his forces, he was entirely defeated. A. D. 1212.

The fame diffenfions, however, which had ruined the Saracens, now broke out among the Chriftians, and enabled the former to fhelter themfelves in Grenada, the only province now remaining to them in Spain. Here they continued till the different monarchies which had been erected on their ruin, were all, except Navarre, united under
A.D. 1492. Ferdinand and Ifabella. Grenada was then taken; but the Moors were allowed to remain in the country, as fubjects, till the reign of Philip
the

the Third, who, in apprehenfion of an infurrection, banifhed them entirely from out of his kingdom.

A.D. 1602.

The depopulation which this meafure occafioned, is fenfibly felt to the prefent day. Count Julian was himfelf put to death by the Moors, on a fufpicion that he intended to defert their caufe. His fate afforded us an ample field for reflection.

We continued our courfe along the Barbary fhore till midnight. We were then obliged to tack, and are now oppofite Malaga, twenty leagues from Gibraltar. This, confidering that the wind has been conftantly eafterly, is no bad fpecimen of our failing.

On the fpot we are paffing, Sir George Rooke, foon after he had taken Gibraltar, engaged the Grand Fleet of France, confifting of fifty-two fail of the line. The Englifh and Dutch had as many fhips;

but the French, being later from port, were much better manned, and in supe-

Auguſt 13, 1704.

rior condition. The battle laſted all the day. Both ſides ſuffered a very ſevere loſs in men; but not one veſſel was taken or deſtroyed. Each claimed the victory; but the French Admirals took care not to face us again during the whole of the war.

Auguſt 8th and 9th.

Calms and light eaſterly winds. The ſea, for ſeveral miles round us, is entirely covered with the ſpawn of fiſh. Philoſophers have not been able to determine how theſe animals are engendered: I will therefore paſs them over. The Grenada mountains riſe to a ſtupendous height on our left, and, even at this late ſeaſon, their heads are covered with ſnow.

Auguſt 10th, Noon.

We have been, all this morning, in ſight of Almeria. The ſhore, for two or three

three leagues on each fide, is almoft flat, with a very fine beach; but the town itself difplays all the variety of hill, dale and water. It ftands on a river, whofe banks feem in high cultivation, and are over-hung by prodigious mountains; whilft the low ground, particularly to the eaft, rifes in a gradual flope, covered with groves and avenues of olive, and cork-trees, interfperfed with vines and green canes. This beautiful fpot forms a kind of amphitheatre, enclofed by the Grenadines, whofe rugged fummits appear almoft inacceffible.

On a fteep afcent, at the Weft end of the town, ftands a large Moorifh caftle, in very good repair. At prefent it is only refpectable for its antiquity; but, in 1147, it made a moft vigorous defence againft Conrad the Third, affifted by the French, Genoefe, and Pifans; and, after a glorious refiftance, it was taken by affault, and all the Moors moft inhumanly put to death.

death. Vaft riches were found in the place, particularly the famous Agate fhip, which is ftill fhewn by the Genoefe, as one of the moft valuable curiofities in Genoa. The caftle of Almeria is an exact copy of that at Gibraltar, and, like it, is commanded by an height immediately above it.

Dufk. Early in the afternoon, a breeze fprang up, and we are now off Cape de Gatt, about fix leagues from Almeria, and fifty-two from Gibraltar. On the point, the Spaniards have a fmall barbette battery. The land, for fome miles on each fide, is almoft perpendicular; but, although we are near a league from the fhore, we have foundings in fixteen fathoms. The eafterly wind continuing, we have juft tacked, and are ftanding to the South.

Auguft 11th.
In the morning, we made Abido, an ifland of rocks, on the Barbary fhore,

Lat.

Lat. 35° 44', Long. 51' W. and, in the afternoon, paſſed between the iſland and the main, which no Britiſh ſhip, I believe, ever did before. The paſſage is barely three leagues wide; but the ſhalloweſt water, three quarters of a mile from the rocks, was thirty-ſeven fathoms. The wind being contrary, we were ſeveral hours in working through.

Auguſt 12th.

During laſt night, we croſſed from the African to the Spaniſh ſhore, where the wind has left us in a calm.

Auguſt 13th, Mid-day.

We are now in ſight of Almazaron, a ſcattered village, at the bottom of a ſmall bay, well flanked by ſome little works on the cliffs on each ſide. At 4 P. M. tacked in fifteen fathoms water, one mile off Cape Tignoſe. On the weſt ſide of this point, there is good anchorage, well ſheltered from the eaſt wind. The Spaniards

have

have a white tower on the point, on which they have mounted two or three small guns; and, indeed, we have scarce seen a spot on the coast of Spain, that a boat could land on, but what is defended by a tower or a little battery. Slight as these works appear, they not only check the smugglers, but have frequently been of service in protecting the coasters from the depredations of the Barbary corsairs; while they also communicate intelligence, by signals, from one extremity of the kingdom to the other, in very few hours.

Tuesday, August 14th.

The wind blowing hard from the East, with a heavy swell, we have anchored off the mouth of Carthagena harbour.

Notwithstanding the adverse winds, nothing could be more pleasant than our voyage. We have crossed the Mediterranean

ranean several times, but have never been more than twelve hours out of sight of land; and the weather, till last night, was so moderate, that not a soul has been sea sick.

The Spaniards have been remarkably civil. They have made a thousand apologies for putting us under quarantine, and have promised to send us every thing we may want. Carthagena is in Lat. 37° 42′, Long. 58′ W. two hundred and fifty miles from Gibraltar. It was built by Asdrubal, from whose country it took its name. I will be more particular in my next letter.

LETTER II.

TO CAPTAIN SMITH.

Carthagena, Auguſt 15th.

MY DEAR FRIEND,

THE entrance of this harbour is not more than ſix hundred yards wide, and is flanked by about thirty guns on the eaſt ſide, and two-and-twenty on the weſt: But, as troops coming from the town, muſt take a conſiderable circuit round the water, I imagine that, on a ſudden attack, theſe batteries would not be manned in leſs than two hours. I can diſcern no embrazures on the line wall towards the ſea; but, on the pier without the gates, there is a low battery of fifty heavy guns, to defend the entrance of the baſon at the weſt end of the town. This paſſage has no defence on the oppoſite ſide, but is ſcarce fifty yards wide. The King's ſhips are laid up immediately within it. At preſent, they amount to

twenty-

twenty-one sail of the line, besides frigates; but they are so closely lashed together, that, if one took fire, the whole, in all probability, would be consumed. None of them are coppered, nor have they any masts standing; and, although Carthagena is the second naval arsenal in Spain, nothing like a man of war in any readiness for service, is here to be seen, except a small copper-bottomed brig, and a few galleys: of these the brig only is in commission *.

The dock-yard is contiguous to the bason, and both are commanded by several heights. Two of these are secured by redoubts; the rest are intrusted to crosses. The works round the city are, I

* This was only four weeks before the French Ambassador delivered the hostile declaration, which, to the honor of our country, his Court was compelled to retract, and proves, that nothing had been pre-concerted with Spain, relative to the succours to be given to the French faction in Holland.

believe,

believe, but weak; and there are several fine landing places within a day's march of the town.

We felt much obliged to the Governor, Don Joseph De Rocas, for his very great attention. Besides repeated offers of his best services, he sent his Aid de Camp to compliment us on our arrival, and to express the utmost regret, that the orders from his Court were so strict, that he could not have the honor of seeing us on shore, until we had performed a tedious quarantine; but, in the mean while, if we were disposed to amuse ourselves in the harbour, he would send a boat to shew us every thing we wished, and would do all in his power, to make our stay as pleasant as possible. We thanked him for his kindness and civility, and, in return, determined to give him no trouble.

As the English were once in possession of Carthagena, and I may have frequent
occasion

occasion to mention the operations of the British arms in the Mediterranean, to prevent repetition, I will recite, in as few words as possible, the rise, progress, and conclusion of the War of the Succession.

Ferdinand and Isabella were succeeded, in 1515, by their grandson, the famous Charles, afterwards Emperor of Germany. Charles, in 1556, resigned his crown to his son, Philip II. whose grandson, Philip IV. had issue, Charles, Maria Theresa, and Margaret. Maria Theresa married Louis XIV. of France, who was compelled to resign every pretension he might afterwards have to Spain, in consequence of this marriage; and Margaret was given to the Emperor Leopold.

Philip IV. was succeeded by his son Charles II. who seemed likely to leave no issue. Louis XIV. therefore apprehending that, at the death of this King, a great contest would arise for the crown of Spain,

Spain, entered into a secret treaty with William III. and the Dutch, for the partition of its dominions: by which it was agreed, that all the Spanish territories in Italy, the province of Guipuscoa in Spain, and the duchies of Lorrain and Bar, should devolve to the Dauphin; whilst the kingdom of Spain, and Spanish America, should be given to the Archduke Charles, the Emperor's second son, the eldest being already provided for. It is to be observed, that these sons were by the Emperor's second marriage, Margaret and all her issue being dead. The Dauphin would therefore have been the undoubted heir apparent, had not his father, on his marriage, renounced his right.

The Spaniards, who were so nearly concerned, knew nothing of this Partition Treaty. Soon after its conclusion, Charles II. of Spain died, and, by his will, left all his dominions to Philip, Duke of Anjou, the Dauphin's second son. Louis immediately

immediately sent his grandson to ascend the throne. This was a breach of the Partition Treaty, which William determined to oppose; but dying at this crisis, war was declared by Queen Anne, who, in conjunction with the Emperor Leopold and the Dutch, set up the Archduke Charles, in opposition to the Duke of Anjou. In this war several other Powers took part.

Sir George Rooke and the Duke of Ormond were sent to Cadiz, in hopes that the Andalusians would declare for Charles: but they refused to acknowlege him; and the English, thinking the town too strong to be carried by force, re-embarked. On their return, Sir George and the Duke, hearing that a squadron of French men of war, with a very valuable convoy, had put into Vigo, determined to attack them; which they executed with the most brilliant success. Ten line-of-battle ships and eleven

Oct. 1702.

eleven galleons were taken, and six galleons and five sail of the line, burnt, besides many smaller vessels.

In 1704, the Archduke embarked on board the Confederate Fleet, and, after an unsuccessful attempt on Barcelona, set off for Lisbon, the Portuguese having espoused his cause against Philip. In the mean while, Sir George took Gibraltar, and engaged Count Thoulouse off Malaga. Gibraltar was immediately besieged by the French and Spaniards, but was relieved by Admiral Leake, in 1705, who took a line-of-battle ship, and burnt four more.

Charles again embarked on board our fleet, at Altea Bay, with Lord Peterborough, and the Prince of Hesse Darmstadt. The Prince was repulsed and killed at the assault of Fort Montjuic, at Barcelona; but Lord Peterborough instantly renewed the attack, and carried the fort. The town surrendered soon

Sept. 3, 1705.

soon after. Lord Peterborough marched directly into Valentia, and, in a few months, with scarce six thousand English troops, overrun the greatest part of Spain, and entered Madrid in triumph. His stay there, however, was but short; for he was obliged to return to the assistance of King Charles, who was now besieged in Barcelona, by General Tessé: but, on the Earl's approach, the French General raised the siege with the utmost precipitation, leaving all his baggage, camp equipage, artillery and wounded men behind him. Victory, throughout this campaign, was the constant attendant on the British arms. The town of Alicant was taken by assault; and the citadel surrendered next day. Carthagena having offered to acknowlege Charles, a detachment was sent to secure it. Majorca and Ivica surrendered soon after.

April, 1706.

June 28.

But the eminent services of the Earl of Peterborough not gaining him a proper influence

influence in the Administration, he resigned his command, and was succeeded by Lord Galway, a brave man. But, by the mismanagement of King Charles, his affairs fell into great confusion; and Lord Galway, being obliged to engage the enemy under many disadvantages at Almanza, was entirely defeated. The consequences of this victory gave Philip a decided superiority in Spain.

April 14, 1707.

In the mean while, the Duke of Marlborough having carried all before him in Flanders, and the Duke of Savoy having driven the enemy out of his dominions, it was resolved, that the army under his Highness's command in Italy, assisted by the fleet in the Mediterranean, should besiege Toulon: but the Emperor Joseph, who had succeeded his father Leopold, withdrawing his forces to besiege Naples, and the French making a successful sally, in which they burnt

August 4.

burnt all the batteries, the Allies were obliged to raife the fiege.

Nothing remarkable was done in Spain in 1708. Our army was reinforced, and the enemy's diftreffed by the capture of a large convoy of provifions. Cagliari, the capital, and the whole ifland of Sardinia, fubmitted to King Charles; Minorca was taken by General Stanhope, and Naples furrendered to the Emperor.

Next year, Alicant was taken by the enemy. The rock on which the citadel ftood, was defended for feveral months, by Major General Richards, with the moft romantic valour, but was at laft undermined and blown up. The General, and moft of the principal Officers, having purpofely expofed themfelves, to animate the garrifon to ftand the threatened fhock, were loft in the explofion; but the furvivors, under Colonel D'Allon, defended themfelves

April, 1709.

till the British fleet arrived and carried them off.

During the remainder of the war, Charles's affairs continued to decline; and his success at Sarragossa and Almanara was balanced by a defeat at Villa Viciosa, and the capture of General Stanhope's army at Brihuega.

At this juncture, his brother died, and Charles, succeeding to the empire of Germany (1711), left Spain; but his partizans, assisted by the English under the Duke of Argyle, kept possession of Barcelona, and the greatest part of Catalonia, till the peace of Utrecht in 1713.

By this treaty, Charles resigned his pretensions to Spain; but, in addition to the empire, he retained Sardinia, Naples, Milan, and the Spanish Netherlands. Sicily was given to the Duke of Savoy, with the title of King; together with
Fenestrelles,

Feneftrelles, and fome other places taken from the French. The Dutch got their Barrier; the Englifh, only Minorca and Gibraltar, with fome fettlements in North America. Pruffia got Upper Gueldres.

Philip, Duke of Anjou, was declared King of Spain: but, to prevent that kingdom and France from ever being united under one head, Philip was obliged to renounce every future claim to France; whilft the Dukes of Berry and Orleans were obliged to do the fame by Spain.

I wifh much to enlarge on the gallant exploits of the Earl of Peterborough, the heroic defence of General Richards, and the noble fpirit of the Catalonians after they were abandoned by the Emperor and Queen Ann to the chaftifement of Philip; but the bounds prefcribed to a journal will not permit me.

LETTER III.

TO CAPTAIN SMITH.

Cagliari, September 1st.

MY DEAR FRIEND,

ON the 16th of laſt month, we weighed anchor off the harbour of Carthagena, and ſailed out of the bay, between the rock and the continent, to the great aſtoniſhment of the Spaniards: but, although one might almoſt ſhake hands with them on each ſide, there is no danger in a ſteady breeze; for the ſhore is ſo bold, that, whilſt we had ſoundings in fourteen fathoms on one ſide of the ſhip, we found no bottom with a line of twenty on the other.

The wind favoured us for ſome hours; but, before night, it got back to its old quarter, the eaſt, and continued there, with little variation, till the 23d. By this time, after having had a diftant view of the high land of Majorca, we were in fight of Sardinia, in Lat. 40° 10′, and, with the affiftance of the land breeze, got down to Cape Tolero on the 24th. In the night, we paffed two rocks, called the Bull and Cow, Lat. 38° 35′, and, on the 25th, anchored in the bay of Cagliari, the capital, Lat. 39° 14′, Long. 9° 20′ Eaft, diftant from Gibraltar about two hundred and fifty leagues.

Early the next morning, we got prattick, with an invitation to dine with the Viceroy, Count St. André. Three carriages were fent to carry us to the palace. The dinner was in the French ftile, and the head difh in the fecond courfe was half a young wild boar, roafted entire: it was fuperior to any pork I ever tafted. We had no wine but at dinner, and one glafs of *liqueur* after the defert. The principal people of the ifland were invited to meet

meet us, and among them, the Marchionesses of Villarias and Pasqua, and the Baroness Tauolard, the three handsomest of their ladies.

Villarias has captured all our hearts. I have often endeavoured to form an idea of Eve in her state of innocence, but never succeeded until I saw this charming *Marchesa*. With the first rank and fashion, she is a child of Nature, and Nature in perfection. Her limbs are most elegantly turned, and her beautiful shape is neither distorted by stays, nor encumbered by a load of false *croupion*. It is impossible to describe how such a woman moves. She is of the middle size, and in the prime of youth. Her face is equal to her person, brunette, with lovely black eyes, whose expression gives full force to the vivacity of her conversation.

Pasqua possesses every attraction but that of drawing one from Villarias. Tauolard

Tauolard is handsome and amiable, but has not so much of *L'Allegro* as the other two. Their dress is like the English; but the unnatural passion for monstrous protuberances, which I am sorry to hear still reigns among our fair countrywomen, hath not yet reached Cagliari.

In their manners, the Sardinian ladies are more like the French. They say every thing that comes uppermost, and have no idea of reserve. You kiss their hands as a mere compliment; and, in dancing, whenever you turn a lady, she expects you to put your arm round her waist, whilst her's rests on your shoulder.

This frankness is vastly pleasant, and is here of no evil tendency; for, in a confined society, secluded from the general world, where the characters and their connections are thoroughly known, and where the number of the profligate is too small to find either countenance or protection,

tection, confidence and sincerity on the part of the women, naturally produce honor and esteem in the breasts of the men.

THE STORY OF LUCILLA.

MOST RESPECTFULLY INSCRIBED TO

The Hon. Mrs. CHETWYND STAPYLTON

AFTER coffee, the ladies carried us to see a nunnery, of which there are no less than fourteen in Sardinia. I have ever thought these institutions a defect in policy, and have reprobated the idea of the Almighty being pleased at our depriving ourselves of the power of doing any one good and moral action: but, in justice to the Superintendants in this island, it must be observed, that no girl is permitted to become a Novice until she is fifteen, and must then serve a year longer before she can be allowed to take the veil; but this ceremony once performed, she must bid an eternal farewel to the world.

We saw none of the Nuns but the Superiors and Novices. They stood within the inner door, which, as a particular distinction, they opened while they conversed with us across the threshold. My attention was soon arrested by the youngest of the Superiors.

She appears scarcely thirty. Confinement has only softened the colour of her cheek, and composed the lustre of her eye. Her features are perfectly regular, and her countenance is animated by the cheerful glow of benevolence and virtue. With the gentleness of a saint, she possesses all the accomplishments of a woman of the world, and speaks a variety of languages, with a voice harmoniously sweet.

Her name is Lucilla. She is aunt to the beautiful Villarias, and, like her, in her youth, was the pride of Sardinia. Early in life, she engaged herself to Fernando, a young a young nobleman, in every refpect her equal. Their hearts were already united, and the day was fixed for their nuptials; but, before this happy hour could be celebrated, the fudden death of the beft of parents obliged Fernando to pafs over to the Continent, to perform the laft offices to his deceafed, and affectionate father. Before his departure, he repeated thofe endearing vows of eternal conftancy, which both he and Lucilla had often given and received; and each promifed to write by every opportunity.

Lucilla kept her word; and when the time fhe expected an anfwer had expired, her mind was filled with anxious fears for her lover's fafety. At length fhe heard of his arrival at Turin from his friends, moft of whom had received letters from him; but Lucilla, who expected to have had the firft, got none. She was too generous to be fufpicious, and, inftead of complaining, continued

writing

writing to Fernando in the moſt affectionate terms, making every excuſe for not hearing from him, but entreating him, as he valued her affection, to write to her by every channel.

The amiable Lucilla had ſtill the mortification of ſeeing poſt after poſt arrive, without a line from her lover. At length ſhe heard, accidentally, that he was ſoon to ſet out for Spain, from whence he was to embark for South America. A thouſand painful emotions now ſeized her breaſt, and her grief for her lover's unworthineſs was not the leaſt. Her fate was drawing to a criſis; and, as her laſt reſource, ſhe wrote him the following letter:

" Until I heard of your preparations
" for croſſing the Atlantic, I attributed
" your ſilence to your confidence in my
" eſteem, and in my unalterable attach-
" ment; and when I reflected how long
" your

"your indispensable concerns would engage you, I had almost persuaded myself to wish that you would not prolong your absence, even by the time in which you would be writing to me: but, what I have hitherto considered as an occasional flight, is now become an injury so cruel and inhuman, that, with all my prejudice in your favor, I have great difficulty to make myself believe that I am not entirely bereft of your affection. If you are capable of such inconstancy, I absolve you of your vows; and may Heaven forgive you. Mine, I shall ever keep sacred. If you deprive me of the power of fulfilling them—the convent of St. Lucia is not far from me: there will I for ever seclude myself from the world, and confirm how sincerely I am your

"LUCILLA."

This letter having only increased her disappointment, Lucilla took the irrevokable

vokable vow, and exerted all her refolution to fubdue her paffion. Two years after fhe had taken the veil, her guardian died; and, in his laft moments, the wretch confeffed, that he had never forwarded any of the letters intrufted to him, and that he had kept Fernando's. He pointed to a box, where they were depofited; but death prevented his difcovering his motive for fuch enormous treachery.

Fernando's letters were exactly in the fame ftrain with Lucilla's. He frequently mentions, that his friends in Spain had folicited him to accept one of the chief appointments in South America; but that he fhould think the whole world itfelf no recompenfe for being abfent from his Lucilla. In his laft, he reminds her of her vows, with the utmoft delicacy and affection. He affures her that, without her, all fituations will be equally miferable to him, and conjures her, in the moft paffionate terms, no longer to trifle with
his

his happiness; for, that he should be obliged to yield to the importunity of his Spanish relations, unless she would again make Sardinia a Paradise, by assuring him of her constancy.

Lucilla was soon informed how cruelly she had been deceived; but, far from complaining, she was almost overcome with joy at the proof of her lover's affection. From that time, she reassumed her former cheerfulness; and, with injuries sufficient to distract any thing less than an angel, I really believe she is the happiest person in the convent. Such are the comforts of religion, and so true is the adage—" Virtue is happiness," that Lucilla's thoughts now rise superior to the world; and, without offending the Deity by heat or impatience, she looks, with tranquil joy, for that moment which will be the commencement of endless bliss, when she and Fernando will be united in Heaven.

I leave

I leave you to conceive, my dear Madam, how much her hiftory increafed the veneration I before felt for her. Villarias is my author. Her words, enforced by her expreffive countenance, are engraven on my heart; but it is impoffible to tranflate them. The youthful Marchionefs is no enthufiaft in favor of nunneries; but fhe has made me allow, that, to difpofitions and misfortunes like Lucilla's, they afford a comfortable afylum.

LETTER IV.

TO CAPTAIN SMITH.

Cagliari, September 1st.

MY DEAR SIR,

THE churches here are plainer than one expects in a Roman Catholic country; but many of them are beautifully neat. The altar-pieces are composed of coloured marble, with no other ornaments than plated candlesticks and artificial flowers. We have seen but few paintings, and very little sculpture. The piece which struck us most, was for its singularity as a religious ornament, in one of the chapels of the cathedral. It is a group, with two figures a little detached on each side; neither of whom convey any idea of decency, much less of religion.

The only proceffion I have feen, I at firft miftook for a recruiting party. It was led by a red ftandard, with drums and fifes playing Malbrook, followed by feveral detachments of menial ecclefiaftics, in party-coloured dreffes, with a fmall crucifix between each divifion. The rear was brought up by an image of the Virgin Mary, and a chorus. Thefe gentlemen were rather fparing of their mufic; but what they did perform, was remarkably fine.

On the fecond night after our arrival, Count André gave us a ball at the palace. The dances were all Englifh, except two: the firft was La Courance; the other, a Sardinian. It confifts of an unlimited number of ladies and gentlemen, who ftand in a ring, and dance feveral times round the centre, in fhort fteps, to a meafure, fomething like the flow time of a *Fandango.* Every now and then, the whole clofe; and the men, with an
imitation

imitation of neighing, firſt kick their legs forward, then throw them back, fall on their knees, and ſpring to their places. The ring now opens, and the two ends turning outwards, lead round till they join. After footing it a little thus back to back, the former manœuvre is repeated, to bring the ring to its original poſition, and the dance is ended. The ball concluded with *Country Bumpkin,* to the great delight of the Sardinians, who had never ſeen it properly danced. I had the pleaſure of dancing that, as well as La Courance, and another with the charming Villarias. Different ices were ſerved between the dances, and we broke up about an hour after midnight. We were introduced to near twenty ladies, but none of them are worth a particular deſcription but the three I have named.

The Viceroy is a man of good underſtanding, and of accompliſhed manners.

He

He was formerly Governor of Nice, and always remarkable for his partiality to the English. One afternoon when we were almoſt *en famille,* he ſaid, " *Allons en Angleterre,*" and led us into another room, where we found a complete tea-table. He was highly pleaſed at the agreeable ſurpriſe he ſaw in our countenances, and we were equally charmed with his flattering attention. He has had ſome of us to dine with him every day, and always ſends his carriages for us. Let this, my dear friend, be a leſſon to us to treat ſtrangers with attention. We are always ſure of receiving it abroad, and it is ſhameful not to return it at home. His ſon, the Chevalier de Revel, poſſeſſes all the politeneſs of the French, with the ſincerity of the Engliſh. He has been in every part of England, and ſpeaks our language very fluently.

Sardinia

Sardinia is now subject to the Duke of Savoy, who by the Quadruple Alliance, A. D. 1720. was obliged to accept it in lieu of Sicily, which was given to the Emperor. It is 140 miles long, and 70 broad, and contains 420,000 souls. The revenue arises chiefly from a duty upon salt, and is barely sufficient to defray its expences; but it certainly might be considerably augmented, as the soil produces wine, corn, and oil in abundance. Most of the salt that is exported, is taken by the Danes and Swedes; the English formerly took great quantities for Newfoundland, but having found the procuring it from Spain and Portugal more convenient, they now take little or none. A profitable tunny fishery is carried on at the south west part of the island, but it is monopolized by the Duke de St. Pierre, and a few more people, who happen to be proprietors of the adjoining land. Wild boars abound in the hilly parts of the island, and here are some

some few deer, not so large as ours, but in colour and make exactly the same. I tasted part of one at the Viceroy's, and found it by no means inferior to our doe venison.

The Feudal System still subsists in a limited degree, and titles go with their estates, so that by purchasing the latter, you inherit the former. The regular troops seldom exceed two thousand men, but the militia amount to near twenty-six thousand, of whom eleven thousand are cavalry. Their horses are small, but uncommonly active. In a charge we should beat them, but on a march they would be superior to us. The country people are generally armed; but notwithstanding their having been so long under the Spanish and Italian government, assassinations are by no means frequent; and yet by the laws of the country, if a man stabs another without premeditated malice, within four hours

after

after quarrelling with him, he is not liable to be hanged. On the other hand, the church affords no protection to the guilty.

The Sardinians are not at all bigoted, and, next to the Spaniards, the Englifh are their favorites In 1708, the Viceroy was difpofed to fupport the Duke of Anjou, but on the approach of the Britifh fleet, the inhabitants obliged him to acknowledge Charles.

The town ftands on the fide of an hill, rifing from the fea, with a rampart round it. The fituation is ftrong by nature; but the works are much out of repair. The worft of this port is, that, on account of the fhoalnefs of the water, men of war are obliged to lay a long diftance from the fhore; and, although the bay is of a very confiderable extent, yet the channel for large fhips is fo narrow,

narrow, that, in working out with a contrary wind, it is difficult to avoid getting aground; but, as the bottom is, in general, foft, touching is attended with no bad confequence but the trouble of getting off.

For feveral leagues round the hill on which Cagliari ftands, the country is almoft flat; but, although it appears remarkably fine, it is reckoned prodigioufly unhealthy; and it is a known fact, that the night air, in many parts of this ifland, is a kind of poifon to ftrangers. The harveft is got in. The grapes are ripe; but the vintage has fcarce begun. The vines are exactly in the order recommended by Virgil. We rode through feveral of the vineyards, and found the peafants exceffively civil. They loaded us with their beft grapes; and it was with the utmoft difficulty, that we prevailed upon them to accept any money in return.

return. They drefs like the Spaniards, to whom they are ftill much attached; and I found my underftanding Spanifh a great recommendation, even with the Nobleffe, and the divine Lucilla.

LETTER V.

TO CAPTAIN SMITH.

Naples, September 9th.

MY DEAR FRIEND,

WE left Sardinia on the 3d inftant; on the 7th, at day-light, were in fight of Mount Vefuvius; and, in the evening, we were clofe to Capria, a fmall ifland on the right of the entrance to the bay of Naples, famous for the abode of Tiberius. In fize and fhape, it is not unlike Gibraltar. The town is in the center of the weft fide, furrounded and interfperfed with vines and evergreens, which give the houfes the appearance of fo many villas peeping through the trees. This fpot is extremely beautiful; but every other part of the ifland is a bare rock.

When Tiberius, from the confciouf-
nefs of his crimes, was in perpetual dread
of being affaffinated, he made choice of
Capria, as a place of fecurity. It is totally inacceffible on every part, except at
a little bay, which he furrounded with
guards, and allowed nobody to enter but
by his own invitation. Here he carried
on the moft abominable debauchery; and
the accounts we read of his brutality are
confirmed by the number of obfcene
medals and paintings found in the town.

That which exhibits the beautiful Malonia can never be beheld but with the
utmoft horror and compaffion. In thofe
vitiated times, this unfortunate lady lived
on terms of the pureft affection with her
hufband, and carefully avoided the Emperor's court. But when, from his age
and infirmities, Tiberius was looked upon
as totally debilitated, he accidentally met
her, and was inftantly ftruck by her
beauty. The modefty of her carriage
only

only increased his desire. She was immediately seized by his guards, and conveyed to the palace, where the horrible monster, finding that neither power nor promises, threats nor severity, could tempt Malonia to swerve from her duty, had a machine contrived to force her to his purpose.—On this she is represented, with a countenance full of anguish and distress. The rest is too shocking to describe.

Passing by Capria, with Vesuvius in front, blazing from time to time during the night, we anchored off Naples the next day, and this morning got prattick.

LETTER VI.

TO CAPTAIN SMITH.

Naples, September 12th.

MY DEAR FRIEND,

WE lost no time in seeing the wonders of this extraordinary country. Our first object was to follow Æneas to the Cuman Shore, and on our way thither, it was but just to pay our oblations at Virgil's Tomb. This celebrated monument is close to the top of the Grotto of Pausilippe, on the left of the east entrance. The inside is a square of twelve feet, with three niches for urns on the east and west sides, two niches and a door, through which you enter, on the south, and the same on the north. The roof is arched, and about nine feet high. The outside was originally octagonal,

gonal, but the angles being worn away, it is now circular, and at a diſtance looks like the remains of a ſmall tower. The materials are of the common kind, and I did not obſerve any marble near it, except two modern inſcriptions.

Formerly the tomb was ſurrounded with laurels, but as every idle viſitor took a leaf, there is not a ſprig left. We could not help exclaiming againſt ſuch ſacrilege; but our guide endeavoured to comfort us, by ſaying that the Marquis Salcitro had ordered a new ſet to be planted.

The Grotto of Pauſilippe is at the weſt end of the ſuburbs of Naples. It is a public road cut through the mountain, near half a mile in length, and wide enough for two carriages to drive abreaſt. Its height is very irregular, in ſome parts eighty feet, and at others only five-and-twenty. In the day time you

you may fee from one end to the other, by the help of two large apertures, cut diagonally from the center of the grotto to the furface of the mount; but at night we were obliged to ufe torches, which, when any number of vehicles are driving together, have a moft beautiful effect. The bottom, like all Naples, is paved with fquare pieces of lava. Its exact date has not been afcertained. The common people infift that it was done by inchantment, as a proof of which they allege that no ftones were found near the entrance. It would be to no purpofe to tell them, that thofe who perforated the mount, very naturally made ufe of the ftone in building the town.

But after all, the difficulty in accomplifhing this paffage was by no means fo great as one would at firft imagine, for the ftone is fo foft, that until it has been for fome time expofed to the air, you may crumble it to duſt. Neither, in my opinion, is this celebrated excavation equal to the batteries, magazines, and communications, formed in the ſolid rock of Gibraltar by Mr. Inch, under the direction of General Eliott, and continued with aſtoniſhing ſucceſs by Major-General O'Hara.

After paſſing the Grotto we drove to Puzzoli. The road is remarkably pleaſant, great part of it runs between groves of poplars, planted in regular order, to ſuſtain the vines, in the ſtyle of our hop gardens. The vines are loaded with grapes, and, encircling the trees, form a variety of beautiful feſtoons from one tree to another in every direction. The ground beneath is either covered with graſs, or laid out for corn.

Turning a little out of the way to the right, we came to Lago D'Agnano, formerly a volcano, now a romantick, beautiful

beautiful lake. Close to it is a little cave called Grotto del Cane, from a vapour that rises in it so obnoxious to dogs, that it kills them in a few minutes, and doubtless it would have the same effect on man, or any other animal, whose head was held near the ground.

Between Lago D'Agnano and Puzzoli, on the side of another extinguished volcano, called the Solfaterra, we saw the Piscatelli, or Boiling Springs, of whose wonderful effect, in turning lava and pumice stone into clay and into soil, I had the same evening the satisfaction of hearing a philosophical account from Sir William Hamilton, with which he has already favoured the public.

We hired a boat at Puzzoli, and after rowing about two miles across part of the celebrated Bay of Baia, with Virgil in my pocket, landed close to the Lucrine Lake, at the foot of Monte Nuovo.

This

This mountain, which is several hundred yards in height, and above a mile in circumference, was thrown up by the Lucrine Lake in a violent earthquake in the year 1538. However strange this may appear, such phenomena are by no means uncommon in Italy. The lake was of course much reduced by this eruption, and now only covers three or four acres. It is about ten yards from the sea, and has a sluice to communicate with it.

After a short walk in a pleasant vineyard, we entered the Sibyl's Cave, a road cut through a mountain in the style of the Grotto of Pausilippe, but on a smaller scale. The passage from the cave to her palace is only wide enough for one person. After descending ten or twelve yards, we came to her baths, four small chambers with water still in them. We were carried through on men's backs, with candles in our hands, and ascending

ing a little on the oppofite fide, came to the door of her palace; but it is fo choaked up with rubbifh, that we were obliged to return without finding an entrance; and paffing through her cave and a wild fhrubbery on the weft of it, we arrived at Lake Avernus, and on the oppofite banks faw the grove where Æneas was to find the golden bough.

The lake feems to have loft the noxious qualities Virgil afcribed to it; but this, I imagine, is owing to moft of the high trees with which it was clofely furrounded being cut down, and little but brufhwood left. The temple is at a fmall diftance on the right of the lake; we wanted to go to it, but our Cicerone perfuaded us that it would be better to delay feeing that and the entrance into Hell, until we had been at Cuma.

We therefore repaſſed the Sibyl's Cave, and returning to the Lucrine Lake, again embarked, and proceeded along the ſhore to the foot of Nero's Palace, where the ſand under the ſea water is ſo hot, that we could ſcarcely touch it. The effect of ſubterraneous fire.

The baths are above. Theſe are ſeveral large chambers, divided into different apartments for the men and women, with two ſubterranean paſſages leading to the water, which unite at the diſtance of two hundred yards from the ſpring. Here the heat is ſo exceſſive and inſupportable, that it is ſuppoſed no longer neceſſary to continue the ſeparate paſſages, ſince even ſhould perſons of different ſexes advance thus far, there is no danger of their being noticed by each other, for to get here coſt us great pain; and all our clothes, in a few ſeconds, were wet through with perſpiration.

This

This is what they call bathing, for nobody can bear the water. One of our guides, for a pecuniary reward, brought a little in a bucket, and boiled some eggs in it, which were afterwards served at our table in a shady spot on the adjoining classic ground; and we crowned this grateful repast with the health of a favorite fair, in a smiling bumper of real Falernian, from the very vineyards which have been celebrated by Horace. The wine was remarkably good, and the heavenly toast gave it a still higher flavour. I am convinced that it would have found its way to England, had not the Italians lost the art of preserving it. One must therefore either drink it new or sour.

About two miles from Nero's Baths, we were shewn the Temple of Diana, a large dome, one half of which was destroyed by an earthquake, the other remains. The Temple of Mercury is on the oppofite fide of a modern bridge. The dome is ftill entire, and is feventy feet in diameter. It has a fimilar effect to the whifpering gallery at St. Paul's. Part of the roof is lined with common mofaic. The walls of the different out-offices are ftill ftanding, and the court has been lately planted with lemon and orange trees, which, in time, will add greatly to the beauty of its appearance. This fpot feems to have been particularly facred, for not an hundred yards further is a large octagon tower, the remains of a Temple of Venus Genetrix, but no other veftige of it is left.

Here we again embarked, and after rowing fome little way along the fhore, landed and walked to the top of a hill, from which we had a view of the Elyfian Fields, and of Lake Acheron below us. The lake is changed, like Avernus, but the Elyfian Fields are ftill a beautiful

tiful wildernefs. On our way we paffed feveral ancient burying-places, and a variety of other ruins—ruins in the trueft fenfe of the word, for the whole is an heap of rubbifh.

A little beyond this is the famous refervoir conftructed for the ufe of the Roman Navy. The roof is fupported by forty-eight fquare pillars, with a proportional number of arches, fomething in the ftyle of the Nun's Ciftern at Gibraltar, but on a fcale fo much more grand, that it would contain above an hundred times the quantity of water.

From thence we proceeded through a vineyard to an amazing fubterraneous building, fuppofed to have been Nero's prifons. The gallery is about twelve feet high, and nine wide. We were told that it proceeds in a right line from the entrance to the fea, and is divided into near an hundred apartments; but

as

as it is full of stones, and as the air is said to be prodigiously hurtful, we could not prevail on our guide to descend to any distance in this direction, but, turning to the left, we entered a range of apartments in the form of a cross, which we supposed were for the officers, as the partition walls are only carried to within two feet of the arch. In the inmost fourteen bronze lamps were found. The niches they stood in still remain. On striking the ground, it returned a hollow sound, as if there was a range of prisons beneath.

As soon as we returned to day-light, we descended to the sea-side, to the tomb of Agrippina. It is an arched vault, fifteen feet long, and nine wide, almost filled up with rubbish. The walls are covered with elegant basso-relievo miniature figures, in small squares, remarkably neat and beautiful; one represents a female deity, with extended wings,

wings, soaring in the air; two others are women reclining on a couch, but so choaked up with smoke and soot from the torches, that it is impossible to determine who they are: the workmanship, however, one easily perceives, exhibits the hand of a capital master, who has displayed so much taste, beauty and harmony, that we are almost tempted to forget Agrippina's crimes; and, in pitying her fate, we redouble our horror at the inhuman parricide who sent her to her tomb.

It is not known by whom this monument was erected; and I think it not improbable, that it might have been ordered by Nero himself, since he is reported to have said, that, had he known how beautiful his mother was, he never would have destroyed her.

Having now seen every thing on the coast of Baia, we returned to Puzzoli, and.

and, to our inexpreſſible concern, found that it was too late to continue our excurſion to Cuma.

Puzzoli abounds with antiquities; but the temple of Jupiter Serapis is the only one we had time to ſee. This was one of the moſt noble ſtructures yet brought to light; and we can never ſufficiently lament, that it has not been preſerved in the ſtate in which it was found.

The court is a ſquare of one hundred and twenty feet, and was ſurrounded by a magnificent colonnade, which, together with the roof and pavement, were of beautiful marble. It contained many elegant ſtatues, and every other religious ornament; but the King was ſeized with ſuch an avidity for theſe treaſures, that he had them all removed to his different palaces, with the exception of four columns only, which are left, as a ſample, before the entrance of the inner temple,

temple, each eighteen feet in circumference, and forty in height. The temple itfelf was again ftopped up with rubbifh, after all its ornaments were taken away.

In the center of the court, an altar was raifed for facrifice; but, as it was compofed of the fineft materials, it was crufhed by the earthquake that buried the temple. The bafe ftill remains, with the ring to which the victim was tied, and the veffels for holding its blood.

LETTER VII.

TO CAPTAIN SMITH.

Naples, September 20th.

MY DEAR FRIEND,

WE returned to Naples, highly gratified with our expedition to Baia, and, after a day's reft, fet out for Mount Vefuvius. The foot of the mountain is about fix miles off. We went at night, in order to view the crater to the greateft advantage, and were about two hours in walking from the bafe to the hermitage. The road, although fteep, is tolerably good; and a light carriage may afcend the greateft part of it.

Father Pietro, the Hermit, received us with great hofpitality; and, although

turned

turned of eighty, he is by no means insensible to those charms of society which are consistent with the gravity of his order. He seemed a person of a liberal education, spoke with great judgment of the ancients, and was well informed of the state of Europe at the time of his retirement. In the course of conversation, he mentioned his having been in England, which led us to enquire in what capacity. Conceive our surprize, when this venerable sage told us that he had been a French hair-dresser! But the frankness and the grace with which he made this declaration, increased our esteem; and his conversation proved, that however low his origin, his abilities and application had raised him superior to most of us.

His habitation is a comfortable cottage, with a chapel, and a shrubbery adjoining, at the extremity of one of the small mountains, of which there are several

several round Vesuvius; and although half way up to the crater, this spot is secured from the lava by a ridge which separates it from the great cone; and should the burning matter run in this direction, it would be thrown on each side. But it is not impossible that he may some day be surrounded by it; and he is always exposed to the stones and ashes thrown up by the mountain.

At three o'clock the next morning we prepared for the grand ascent, but it rained so hard that our guide assured us it was impossible to proceed; and, to our infinite disappointment, the weather did not clear up till after daylight. We then took leave of our friendly hermit, and after scrambling over large fields of rough lava, in less than two hours reached the crater—an unfathomable fiery gulph, sunk from the summit of a monstrous cone, which rises above every other branch of the mountain. It emits an amazing column of smoke, so strongly impregnated with sulphur, that it was not without danger of being suffocated, that we were able to look down it, even on the side from which the wind blew.

The smoke and daylight prevented our seeing to any depth, but at night I imagine that we should occasionally have discerned fire at the bottom. We repeatedly heard a rumbling noise, not so much like that of thunder, as of a brazen carriage rolling over a bridge. These were succeeded by small explosions, which threw up large quantities of stones, accompanied by a flame, which the light prevented our seeing to advantage.

Whilst the mountain is in this dangerous state, it is impossible to measure the circumference of the crater exactly, but I am led to think that it has been exaggerated, and that it does not exceed three hundred yards. Its fides however fometimes fall in, and then the circumference may be much greater.

Figure to yourfelf what a volume of fmoke may be emitted from fuch a fource, and what an overwhelming torrent of liquid fire fuch a gulph may produce! Our fhoes were burnt in getting to its edge, for it is furrounded either with new lava, or a hot, droffy fubftance powdered with fulphur.

Sometimes the mountain is perfectly quiet for weeks together, but it has been fmoking ever fince we arrived, with occafional explofions, which threaten an approaching eruption. There was a flight one a few days before we entered the bay, but the lava only defcended about a mile from the crater. It is ftill

red

red hot, and at night may be seen at many leagues diftance.

The phenomena of lava and burning mountains have been varioufly explained by different philofophers. Some, and thefe men of reputation too, have followed the idea of the ancients, and fuppofe the center of the earth to be fire, to which they are fo extravagant as to imagine volcanos are the chimneys. Others fuppofe them to be occafioned by the fermentation of fireftone, fulphur, and iron, the explofions of nitre, of aqueous fteam violently heated, or of air pent up and greatly rarefied. All thefe doubtlefs affift, or contribute to the formation of volcanos, but the only inexhauftible fource of fire that I am informed of, is the electric fluid, whofe powers were not difcovered before the middle of this century. This is nothing more than the light of the fun abforbed by the earth, which of courfe muft be

again

again emitted, juft as we receive in rain, the water and the damps he exhales from us. Whenever, therefore, the electric fluid is abforbed in larger quantities than the general outlets can return, it acts with uncommon violence, and breaks forth either by an earthquake, or an eruption. When this happens, and the eruption is not very violent, the burning matter rifes gradually from the bottom to the top of the crater, and when it has filled it, it runs over like the boiling of an immenfe caldron. But fometimes it fcorns all bounds, and the crater, monftrous as it is, being infufficient to give vent to its violence, the fide of the mountain is burft open, and thrown with inconceivable force to an immeafurable height in the air. The lava then rufhes forth in an impetuous torrent of liquid fire, overwhelming every thing in its courfe. That of 1767 was fix miles long and two wide, and in fome places, where it paft over cavities,

vities, it was sixty or seventy feet deep.

Eruptions are generally preceded and closed by an immense discharge of stones and ashes, which often create more destruction than the lava itself.

For some time after the eruption, the lava has the appearance of melted glass, after which the upper part breaks into large pieces of a kind of dross, which, in the course of time crumble into mould, and form the richest soil imaginable, whilst the lower becomes hard stone. But this is the process of many years, and consequently great part of Vesuvius is horridly barren, whilst the rest is most beautifully cultivated.

A fog deprived us of the view from the top of the mountain; but, by what I saw at the Hermitage, I think it would have been impossible to describe it. The bay

bay of Naples is upwards of fifty miles in circumference, and the variety of curious and beautiful objects, which strike the eye in every direction, render it one of the most pleasing and interesting sights which it is possible to behold. The capital of the kingdom is in the center, with a superb Carthusian monastery, and the Castle of St. Ilmo above it. On the west the public walk of the Chiaja, adorned with several elegant fountains, and a double row of trees. Beyond it Mount Pausilippe, with the Tomb of Virgil; the road and town of Puzzoli; the Solfaterra, and Monte Nuovo; the remains of the Lucrine Lake, and the ruins of Baia, bounded by the celebrated Cape of Misenus, and the Isle of Ischia. On the east the gardens, palace, and museum of Portici, built over the ruins of Herculaneum, Mount Vesuvius throwing forth an amazing volume of smoke in a variety of shapes, according to the wind, with its base

covered

covered with vineyards, convents, and villas, rifing out of the afhes of Pompeia and Stabia. Beyond thefe Caftello Mare, clofed by the Promontory of Gampenela, and the Ifland of Capria. The whole country is in the higheft ftate of cultivation, richly clothed with beautiful trees, moft of which are evergreens.

The entrance of the bay is on the fouth-weft fide, and is near fifteen miles wide. Off the town there are two moles, one for the King's galleys, the other for the larger men of war and merchantmen, with three caftles to defend them. But notwithftanding thefe works, and the Citadel of St. Ilmo, which, from its height, is unaffailable, and that its garrifon is fheltered by excellent cafemates, I think ten fail of the line might lay this capital in afhes, as a firft rate man of war may lie clofe to the fhore.

By

By Sir William Hamilton's defire, we, this morning, took a boat from the Pearl, and after rowing along the weſt ſide of the town, and paſſing the ruins of Queen Joan's Palace, landed at a ſmall village, he was ſo good as to point out to us, in the neighbourhood of which we ſaw the remains of Pollio's Villa, with the ſubterranean fiſh-ponds, in which he uſed to feed lampreys on human fleſh. There are ſome buſts of his family in the garden, and ſeveral inſcriptions to remind us of his abominable luxury.

LETTER VIII.

TO CAPTAIN SMITH.

Naples, September 24th.

MY DEAR FRIEND,

ON a hill, a little without this city, the King has a palace, called Capo de Monté, in which there is a museum, and a numerous collection of paintings, the best of which is Titian's celebrated Danaæ. Nothing can be more beautiful, or expressive of enjoyment, than her face, or more elegantly shaped than her person: but, dared I suppose it possible to improve the design of so perfect a master, I would say, that, for Jupiter's sake, I wish that her knees were less drawn up.

Scidon's Charity is a divine figure, and, if poffible, exalts that heavenly virtue.

The Dead Chrift, by A. Carraccio; Mary Magdalen, by Giucino; Peter denying Chrift, by Morillo; the Virgin Mary, with St. Ann, Jefus, and John the Baptift, by Raphael, are among the beft pieces.

The mufeum contains a complete fet of medals in gold, filver and copper, of all the Roman Emperors; a variety of beautiful cameos, antique vafes, and a copy of the Farnefe Bull.

Our next grand object was to vifit the recovered towns of Herculaneum and Pompeia, which, after being buried near feventeen hundred years, were again brought to light by the prefent * King of Spain, whilft he was on the throne of Naples.

* Died on the 13th of December, 1788.

These towns were lost in the reign of Titus, by the memorable eruption of Vesuvius, in the year of our Lord 79, when the mountain threw forth such a torrent of stones and lava, that Herculaneum and Stabia were buried near eighty feet deep in ashes, consolidated by liquid fire.

In the revolution of so many ages, the spot they stood upon was entirely forgotten: but, towards the end of the last century, some inscriptions were found, which led to a discovery of their situation; but it was not till the year 1738, that any public excavations were made.

The King met with so much success in his first attempt, that, notwithstanding the expence of digging through sixty or eighty feet of hard stone, he laid open a considerable part of Herculaneum; but the difficulty of removing the rubbish induced his Majesty to fill it up again

again as he went on, after collecting all the moveables of any confequence. The theatre alone is left open. It is larger than any in England; and the ends of the beams, burnt to coal, are ftill feen fticking in the walls; but all the ornaments that withftood the eruption are removed to Portici.

No lava having ever gone over the afhes which buried Pompeia, it was much eafier cleared. Three divifions are quite open. The firft is a fmall fquare, which, our Cicerone told us, was the foldiers quarters. There are feveral fmall apartments round it; in one of which we faw the fkeletons of feventeen poor wretches, who were confined by the ancles in an iron machine. Many other bodies were found, fome of them in circumftances which plainly fhew that they were endeavouring to efcape when the eruption overtook them. Near the barracks, there is a theatre, and a temple
of

of Isis; but, as all their ornaments have been removed, they have now little but their antiquity to make them worth seeing.

But a little farther, two streets, with all their houses, are entirely cleared, and look like a small town, lately abandoned. The streets are just wide enough for two carriages to pass each other; and the ruts worn by the wheels, are still to be seen, as well as names, and several military figures, cut in a rough manner by the soldiers on the walls of their quarters. A path is raised on each side of the street, for foot passengers.

Most of the houses have a terrace at top, in the Italian style; and some of them have baths and stoves to heat the walls. The floors, in general, are paved with mosaic of the common kind; and the sides of the rooms were all ornamented with paintings on the bare plaster,

plaster, which we call *in distemper*. Some of them are exceedingly beautiful; but most of the best have been taken away. Among those that remain, the most striking are, Narcissus pining for his own figure; Orpheus and Eurydice; Diana and Endymion; variety of dogs and game; several dishes of fish, fowl and vegetables; a capital helmet; some beautiful landscapes, and light festoons of the most elegant patterns: all as perfect as the day they were painted.

A little without the gates, we saw the burying-place of the Terentian family. It is a small pile, with a tower in the center, with niches for the urns, and several distorted, weeping faces on the walls. In one of the wells in the town, we found several skulls, which were thrown there when the houses were cleared out.

About a quarter of a mile farther, we came to a noble villa, which, from

its

its fize, and the furniture found in it, muft have belonged to fome perfon of confequence. The lower part is inhabited by fome peafants, who cultivate the garden within the court, and who prefented us with fome of the grapes which it produces. The cellars form three fides of a fquare, under the terrace in front of the houfe, each fide one hundred and fixty feet long. We were fhewn feveral jars, whofe contents were folid, and which, at the time of the eruption, were full of wine.

From hence we drove to Portici, to fee the mufeum, where every thing taken out of Pompeia and Herculaneum is collected. It confifts of fixteen rooms, in which the different articles are arranged with very great tafte. The floors are paved with mofaic, taken up from the recovered towns, and the walls of the court are lined with infcriptions.

G. Exclufive

Exclusive of busts and statues, medals, and intaglios, lamps and tripods, innumerable; there is not an article used by the ancients, of which a specimen may not be seen in this museum. We were shewn some Household Gods, and every implement used in worship, or sacrifice, agriculture, and cookery. A kitchen completely furnished, in a style that would do justice to a London Alderman. Several scales, weights, and measures, and different instruments of music and surgery. Some loaves of bread, with the maker's name. Different kinds of shell fruit. Tickets of admission for the theatre, and, what rather lessened our veneration for the ancients, some loaded dice, and a box of rouge. They had mirrors too, which were of brass highly polished, for they had not the art of making glass reflect by quicksilver.

One of the apartments is filled with obscene devices, particularly rings, which
were

were worn by the chafteft matrons, as charms againft fterility; for the Romans accuftomed their women to this kind of objects, juft as they did their youth to danger, that they might learn to behold them unmoved. This accounts for the very great number that have been found. Some of them are highly laughable. But the moderns have learned more delicacy; and this apartment is never expofed to the ladies.

The *Satyr and She Goat* was thought fo dangerous a reprefentation, that it was very properly removed to a feparate houfe; and nothing but its exquifite workmanfhip prevented its being deftroyed.

It is much to be lamented that the article which might be of moft fervice to mankind, is the moft difficult to be recovered, I mean the ancient books. Thefe were written on fcrolls rolled up, and

and by the heat of the aſhes, were burnt into the appearance of charcoal. No pains have been ſpared to unfold them, but the operation is attended with ſuch immenſe difficulty, that as yet but four have been brought to light, and theſe in ſo mutilated a ſtate, that though the letters which are left are perfect, I fear they can never be of any real uſe. But this by no means leſſens the merit of Padre Piaggi and his pupils. It is miraculous that they have ſucceeded ſo well; and their ingenuity and perſeverance cannot be too much applauded.

Several of the rooms in the Palace of Portici, which is adjoining to the muſeum, are lined with the paintings cut out of Pompeia; but though they are reckoned the beſt, they do not appear to me to equal thoſe that remain on their native walls.

The equestrian statues of Marcus Nonius Balbus, and his son, at the foot of the great staircase, are both remarkably light and elegant. One has the greater pleasure in admiring them, from their being a tribute to virtue, erected after their death by the citizens of Herculaneum, of which they were Proconsuls.

Portici is about six miles from Naples, at the foot of Vesuvius; the theatre of Herculaneum is a little beyond the Palace, and Pompeia about seven miles farther, all on the great road to Castello Mare. No excavations having been made at Stabia, we did not go there.

LETTER IX.

TO CAPTAIN SMITH.

Naples, September 27th.

MY DEAR SIR,

ENGAGEMENTS in Naples, which we could not decline, and the shortness of our stay, allowed us to make but one more excursion to the country. This was to the new palace at Casertta. The outside has nothing to boast of but the grandeur of its size; but for convenience, the plan is, perhaps, the best which has ever been laid out. It is a square of six hundred feet each side; and that no room may be lost, the interior court is divided into four, by a range of buildings in the shape of a cross, the head of which forms a most

mag-

magnificent church, lined with the marble from the Temple of Serapis at Puzzoli. It hath not many paintings, but that of the Prefentation is reckoned ineftimable. I do not mean to criticife this admirable work, but it is natural to imagine that the painter intended the Virgin Mary to be his principal character, and yet, in fpite of myfelf, my attention was conftantly drawn from her to the furrounding figures.

The great ftaircafe forms one of the fineft *coup d'oeils* of the kind I ever beheld. It is in the center of the whole edifice, oppofite the church gates. The dome is painted with Apollo and the Mufes, in a circle, and the four feafons in the corners. The fteps and baluftrade are all of marble of different colours, on a very grand fcale, crowned with two capital lions. If any fault can be found with this elegant piece of architecture, it is that the area below is too small in proportion to the grandeur of this part of the building.

It is intended that this Palace shall contain apartments for all the Officers of State, &c. who by the skill of the architect, will be most conveniently lodged; as yet, however, none but those of the King are completed. These are finished in the richest style, and with a neatness and elegance that prevents our being dazzled by their magnificence. The walls are washed with light colours (for the Italians use no paper), with elegant mouldings of gold and silver, and the ceilings are adorned with a variety of most beautiful paintings. That of the Three Graces in the Queen's bath, is a most masterly piece; they have just been bathing, the beauty of their faces and symmetry of their persons, are beyond description.

Several

Several of the lower rooms are filled with statues, not yet put up. The best is Agrippina sitting on a chair, with her feet out, so very natural, that I was on the point of bowing to her. The Theatre is nothing extraordinary. The aqueduct we had not time to see.

St. Januarius is the tutelar saint of the Neapolitans. His feast is now celebrating. The people out of doors affect to laugh at the idea of his blood liquifying; but when the pretended miracle was performed, all of them kissed the phial with great fervour. The *Nobile* have given an oratorio in honor of him; Sir William Hamilton sent us tickets for it.

During this festival the operas are suspended; which has prevented our seeing more than two. The Theatre of St. Carlos, performers, dresses, &c. are,

are, in every respect, superior to ours; and yet, instead of half-a-guinea, the price of admittance is only about eighteen pence.

In England, the singers are never obliged to exert themselves for any time together: here I have heard *La Banti* in a cantata that hath required a constant exertion for near half an hour; *Tomeone*, though less powerful, is more pleasing: in *Pace caro mio Sposo*, she is absolutely incomparable. The Coltalines make too many faces; and this is often the case with the men; but, however hideous in private parties, it is not much observed on the stage. Their dances are longer than ours, and, when they form part of the piece, are accompanied by voices.

It would be presumption to attempt to describe the manners of the Italians on so short an acquaintance. Suffice it to say,

say, that we have been treated with the utmost attention; that the people are remarkably partial to our nation; and that being an English Officer is a sufficient introduction to the first company.

If the lower sort have sometimes taken advantage of our inexperience, it is no more than we have suffered at home; for, who are more imposing, particularly to foreigners, than the publicans, waiters, and all that class of people, in England?

In short, I should be apt to give a very high character of the Neapolitans, had I not been told that they do not merit the favorable opinion I have formed of them, and that the civility of the men often ends in winning your money, whilst that of the women proceeds from an amorous disposition, tinctured with avarice: but all this it would be ungenerous to believe, since we have not experienced an instance of either.
The

The frailty of women I can pity, as well as condemn: but how a lady can fell her virtue, is, though perhaps it may be accounted for here, what Englishmen I hope will never comprehend.

The Princess Belmonté is particularly entitled to our regard. Her fortune renders her superior to any sordid views; and yet she has always been remarkable for the kindest attention to our countrymen. Her Highness invited us to a party at her casino, and shewed us a room entirely furnished in the English style, with the best productions of Bunbury, Hamilton and Strange.

We have been at several *converfazioni*, which, in the principal houses, include every other amusement. A suit of rooms is thrown open; the largest for a promenade in summer, and dancing in winter; the next for music; a third for billiards; a fourth for fruit, ices, &c. and

the

the reſt for cards and dice. But, if only four or five people meet together, the Italians call it a *converſazione.*

The Court has been at Caſtello Mare ever ſince we arrived. We mean to call there on our way out of the bay ; and Lord Hervey, from whom we have received the greateſt civilities, has promiſed to accompany us. His Lordſhip is one of the King's moſt intimate friends; and Lady Hervey, whoſe gentleneſs and good ſenſe inſure her the hearts of all thoſe who have the honour to approach her, is particularly eſteemed and reſpected by the Queen, and all the Italian nobility.

I mentioned before, that the Spaniards ceded Naples to the Emperor, by the Treaty of Utrecht; but Philip V. of Spain's ſecond wife, Elizabeth Farneſe, heireſs to the Duke of Parma, giving him a pretence for invading Italy, in her right,

right, he made a conqueft of Sicily and Naples: but the other European Powers obliged him to form them into a feparate kingdom, and to give it to Charles, his eldeft fon by the Princefs of Parma.— A. D. 1735.

All Philip's children by his firft marriage dying without iffue, Charles fucceeded to the crown of Spain, and re-
A.D. 1759. figned Sicily and Naples to his third fon, Ferdinand IV. the prefent King, the eldeft being an ideot, and the fecond becoming Prince of the Afturias, and heir to Spain.

The government, being founded on conqueft, is of courfe defpotic. The King generally keeps up near thirty thoufand men, who feem to be tolerable troops. The officers are obliged to have a public military education, and are aftonifhed that this is not the cafe with us. The navy confifts of three two-deckers,

deckers, about a dozen frigates, and twenty galleys. They are at war with the Algerines, but feldom take a prize.

The revenue of the King of Naples is near a million fterling. When fupplies are wanted, his Majefty has only to iffue an edict, mentioning the caufe, and the manner in which they are to be raifed. He generally fays, that it is by the defire of his Council, which only confifts of his principal Minifters, and the Queen, who is allowed a confiderable fhare in the adminiftration of the kingdom, from its independence being in a manner obtained through the female line, as I conjecture; for the fhort time I have been in this country has not permitted me to make myfelf mafter of its laws, which, as well as feveral other matters, I muft pafs over till my return. As to churches and convents, I will not detain you with any account of them; for they are nearly

nearly alike in moſt Roman Catholic ſtates.

Naples is in Lat. 40° 53', Long. 14° 12' Eaſt, and, by the ſhorteſt courſe, about a thouſand miles from Gibraltar.

LETTER X.

TO CAPTAIN SMITH.

Off Salerno, October 2d.

MY DEAR FRIEND,

LORD Hervey and Captain Barnard, who have had the goodness to accompany us thus far, being about to leave us, I embrace this opportunity of sending you a continuation of my Journal; a form of writing, which, in conformity to your wishes, I shall always prefer whenever we are at sea.

Friday, September 28th.

At four o'clock, yesterday afternoon, we got under way, in order to pay the King of Naples a visit a Castello Mare. We were becalmed all night; and his Majesty,

Majesty, being apprized of our approach, came out to meet us at day-break, this morning. He was in a man of war brig of fourteen guns, attended by another of the fame force. As foon as he was within about two miles, he got into his barge, and, there being but little wind, rowed on board us. We received him with a royal falute.

His Majesty went all over the ship, praifed every part of her, feemed much pleafed, and, with a moft engaging condefcenfion, thanked us for the honor we did him, and invited the principal perfons on board to dine at his cafino. On leaving the ship, he was again faluted with twenty-one guns.

Immediately afterwards his Majesty fent the officers a prefent of fome very fine fifh of his own catching, and in the afternoon rowed out again to take another view of the ship.

Caftello

Caſtello Mare is the King's dockyard. Every thing is in high order; but it is entirely defencelefs, and does not give an Englifhman a very formidable idea of the Neapolitan Navy.

There is a village adjoining, above which the King has built a fmall palace, or cafino, in a moſt charming fituation, with a full view of the bay. Here his Majeſty generally fpends great part of the fummer, and enjoys his favorite amufements of fifhing and fhooting, water parties, and fhip-building.

The King of Naples is thirty-fix years old, well made, and rather tall; lean enough to enjoy all his diverfions, of a fair complexion, light hair, and an affable, open countenance.

Notwithſtanding the heavy taxes requifite to the fupport of his navy and army, he is adored by his fubjects, from the confidence he repofes in them, and becaufe, in affairs of ftate, he is always their champion. But if he has fometimes fuffered his partiality for the Queen to get the better of his judgment, his people are fenfible that love always predominates in the moft generous breafts.

Her Majefty is a year younger than her hufband. She is fifter to the Emperor of Germany, and to the Queen of France, and is accufed of being extremely ambitious, which the King's eafy temper, by giving her the afcendency in politics, rather increafes. In her youth fhe muft have been amazingly handfome; for notwithftanding her having eight children living, there is ftill fomething very ftriking about her; and her charms, it is faid, are as powerful as ever on the King. There is no believing half the ftories one hears; and when they tend to fcandal or immorality, it

is

is unjuft to repeat any on mere report.

In the evening we got under way, and with a light breeze failed out of the Bay of Naples, between Capria and Cape Gampenela.

September 29th.
Becalmed on the coaft of Salerno. Nothing can be more beautifully picturefque. From the water's edge to the tops of the mountains, not a vacant fpot is to be feen. The whole face of the country is covered with vines, trees, and houfes, mixed together in the prettieft confufion imaginable.

In the afternoon we landed; but the people being fufpicious of us, we could not gain admittance to any of their houfes for a confiderable time. At length a prieft, after having carefully examined us from his miranda, opened his doors, treated

treated us with great hospitality, and laughed at the ignorance of his people.

September 30th.

The Island of Capria is still in sight. Passed the Bay of Salerno, and the wind being light and contrary, brought to off Pestum. Went on shore to examine the ruins.

This ancient city, which flourished before the foundation of Rome, was destroyed by the Goths on the decline of the Roman Empire, and in their zeal for the christian religion, these fierce barbarians overturned every place of Pagan worship exposed to their ravages.

The arch of the east gate of the town is still standing. But of a multitude of beautiful temples, not a column of any one is left, except of three, which

being

being compofed of common ſtone, the barbarians were fatisfied with deſtroying the roofs. Two of thefe are clofe to each other. The one has nine columns in front, and eighteen on each fide; the other has fix by fourteen. Each of the columns is fix feet in diameter, and the fpace between them is eight feet. Both of thefe temples are of the Doric order. The third is of the Corinthian. They are all three noble edifices, and the columns, with a great part of the entablature, are ſtill perfect. Signor Pitelli, a painter whom we brought from Naples, is bufily employed in taking plans of them.

The walls of the city are above two miles in circumference, and eighteen feet thick, and are eafily traced, as well as the mole, which the fea by an earthquake has left dry.

In the middle of the town there was a famous amphitheatre, one hundred and twenty-eight feet in length. Enough of the ground work is left to give a juſt idea of its conſtruction; and the entrance, with arched paſſages on each ſide for the wild beaſts, is ſtill tolerably perfect.

October 1ſt.

Signor Pitelli not having finiſhed the plans, and the wind continuing contrary, we carried him on ſhore again to-day. Here, in a farm-houſe, amidſt theſe ruins of antiquity, we ſaw the modern method of drying figs, and making raiſins. The operation is very ſimple. Expoſe the fruit to the ſun for eight or ten days, then bake it, and when packing up, ſprinkle a little flour between the layers.

Peſtum

Pestum was founded by one of those Grecian colonies, who, in the early ages, established themselves in Italy, whence this country derived the appellation of Magna Grecia.

LETTER XI.

October 2d.

LORD Hervey took leave of us this morning off Salerno, and had scarce made the shore in a boat that attended his Lordship, before we were attacked by an adverse gale of wind, which obliged us to stand towards the west, pretty close to Capria, and, I assure you, it is with no small satisfaction, that we find ourselves sufficiently to windward to fetch the Bay of Naples, should the storm increase.

October 3d.

The gale having moderated, we tacked at one A. M. and at noon the wind became

came fair, but has left a heavy sea against us.

October 4th.

At eight A. M. were in sight of Strombolo, the most northern of the Lipari Islands, which are supposed to be of volcanic origin, that is, thrown up by eruptions occasioned by fire under the sea, whence Virgil makes them the residence of Vulcan.

They are also supposed to have given rise to the fable of Eolus, from one of their Kings of this name, who, by attending to the smoke of the neighbouring islands, had learned to foretell how the wind would blow.

Homer carries Ulysses to Lipari, the capital of that monarch, who, compassionating his sufferings, made him a present of the different winds confined in separate bags, that he might use them

at

at his pleasure; but when they got in sight of Ithaca, his companions, ignorant of the contents, untying the adverse ones, he was driven back in a violent storm, and thus renewed his former woes.

The case is different with us: calms and light variable breezes have kept us in sight of Strombolo the whole day. The volcano is on its south-west side, in so fortunate a situation for the inhabitants, that they have little to fear from eruptions; for the crater is about one fifth of the height of the island below its summit, and is surrounded on every side but that nearest the sea, by large cliffs, which seem to overhang it on purpose to check the eruption when it takes any other direction; for the stones and ashes which it casts forth, rebounding from the rocks above, are either again swallowed up, or thrown down the south-west side into the ocean.

In the afternoon, there was an explosion like the springing of a small mine. The smoke occasioned by this, being quickly dispelled, it resumed its former state, which, at the distance of five leagues, appeared exactly like that which issues from a large double chimney. At this time it bore S. S. E.

At dusk, it looked like a lime-kiln, and every three or four minutes emitted a flame, which blazed for a few seconds like a furnace on fire.

During the night, it appeared in all its glory, with every symptom of an approaching grand eruption. The crater seemed full of burning matter, boiling on its surface, and every now and then throwing up a large column of red-hot stones, which bounded down the side of the mountain into the sea, and, in a manner setting fire to the air as they flew through it, formed one of the
grandest

grandeſt ſights it is poſſible to conceive. The beautiful effect of theſe flying red-hot rocks was not loſt until they had been ſome ſeconds under water.

Formerly there were only ſeven of theſe iſlands, now there are eleven; and, from the active ſtate of Strombolo, which is conſiderably detached from the reſt, I ſhould not be ſurpriſed to hear that another iſland was thrown up near it: but ſuch an event, although often reported, I can aſſure you, has not lately happened here. The laſt phenomenon of this kind that has been thoroughly authenticated, is in the Archipelago, which, in a few weeks, I hope to viſit.

All the Lipari iſlands have had volcanoes in their time; but moſt of them have been extinct for many centuries. The whole are ſubject to the King of Naples, and add a conſiderable ſum to his revenue, from the trade they carry on on in wine, alum, sulphur, and dried fruit. The wine is famous; I tasted some of it at Naples, but did not think it equal to its reputation.

Friday, October 5th.

At day-break, Strombolo was two leagues astern. It looks like a huge rock rising boldly out of the sea, seems to be about twelve miles in circumference, and has a small town on the south-east side. The coast of Calabria, and of Sicily, also in sight. Latitude, at mid-day, 38° 37'.

At sun-set, we entered the celebrated straits of Scylla and Charybdis, and, in less than an hour and a half, anchored at Messina.

LETTER XII.

TO CAPTAIN SMITH.

Meſſina, October 8th.

MY DEAR FRIEND,

MESSINA, which was formerly in ſo flouriſhing a ſtate, and which was accounted one of the prettieſt cities in the world, is now exactly in the condition of Gibraltar during the ſiege; and the inhabitants live in juſt ſuch miſerable places as the huts of Black-town and Windmill-hill.

The front of the town extended along the water ſide, for above two thouſand yards, in the form of a creſcent, adorned with pilaſters and pediments, and a grand eſplanade open to the sea,

sea, which at once formed a noble pier, and a delightful public walk, flanked by a fort at each end. The houses were built with great taste, all four stories high, and nearly alike.

Of this beautiful and magnificent range, only the outside shell remains; the rest, with all the town, except one or two of the strongest churches, was entirely destroyed by the dreadful earthquake in 1783.

The center of that tremendous convulsion was at Oppido, in Calabria. Every thing within twenty miles was entirely overwhelmed, and several towns, with all their inhabitants, completely swallowed up, not the smallest vestige of them being left. Scarce a place within seventy-two miles of Oppido but felt the shock. By the return made to the Secretary of State, the number of people lost, amounted to thirty-two thousand, three hundred and sixty-seven souls; and we were told by Sir William Hamilton, that there were several thousand strangers, travellers, &c. who were not included in that return.

It is by no means uncommon to hear of the Italians scourging their saints when they are overtaken by any misfortune; but, since this dreadful calamity, St. Agatha, the Protectress of Sicily, is more venerated than ever; for, notwithstanding the loss of their property, she has the credit of having defended her votaries from the catastrophe with which their neighbours on the opposite coast were overwhelmed; and every Sunday night the opera ends with a little piece in her honor.

There is something so amiable in this universal gratitude and thanksgiving in the midst of absolute ruin, that it is impossible not to admire the minds that

are

are capable of such virtue, even though actuated by superstition. But, indeed, if we compare Messina with several other places, we may reckon her peculiarly fortunate, since, though the town is destroyed, only nine hundred people perished.

At the time of the earthquake, the Messinians had scarce recovered from the ravages of the plague of 1743. This second blow has completely broken their spirit, and obliged them to relinquish the hope of ever seeing their city rebuilt; the King of Naples having ordered that none of the houses in the Crescent shall be roofed, until they are raised to their former height. The inhabitants have remonstrated, by saying, that they cannot bear the expence; but his Majesty is unwilling that they should lose so beautiful an ornament.

Even Scylla and Charybdis have been almoſt ſubdued by the repeated convulſions of this part of the earth, and by the violence of the current, which is continually increaſing the breadth of the Straits. If proper allowance be made for theſe circumſtances, we ſhall acquit the ancients of any exaggeration, notwithſtanding the very dreadful colours in which they have painted this paſſage. It is formed by a low peninſula, called Cape Pelorus, ſtretching to the eaſtward on the Sicilian ſide, immediately within which lies the famous whirlpool of Charybdis, and by the Rocks of Scylla, which a few miles below on the Calabrian ſhore, project towards the weſt. The current runs with ſurpriſing force from one to the other alternately in the direction of the tide, and the tides themſelves are very irregular. Thus, veſſels by ſhunning the one were in the utmoſt danger of being ſwallowed up by the other.

At

At present, in moderate weather, when the tide is either at ebb or flood, boats pafs all over the whirlpool, but, in general, it is like the meeting of two contending currents, with a number of eddies all around. And, even now, there is fcarcely a winter in which there are not fome wrecks.

At the time we paffed the ftrait, the weather was as favourable as we could wifh, and yet, in fpite of a ftrong breeze and the current, which hurried us on with furprifing velocity, the fhip's head was fuddenly whirled round near three points; but the wind blowing frefh, in a few feconds fhe dafhed through the eddy that had caught her—for, to avoid Scylla, and fecure Meffina, we had kept pretty clofe to Charybdis.

The entrance of these straits is, I am convinced, not less than three miles wide, but I have never heard it allowed to be so much. After passing Charybdis, the sea immediately widens, but Cape Pelorus and Scylla in a manner crossing each other, the passage cannot be perceived until you are on the point of entering it, which gave rise to a tradition, that Hannibal, fancying himself betrayed and land-locked, put his Pilot Pelorus to death; but that, as an atonement, he afterwards erected a statue to his memory, from which the Cape took its name. This action, however, is so contradictory to the history, experience, and disposition of Hannibal, that nobody could ever have raised such a story, but one who had never read the life of this magnanimous hero.

Few countries have experienced more revolutions than Sicily; the richness of the soil and the temperature of the climate, added to its commanding situation, having always made it an object of attraction. After the dark ages it was successively possessed by the Greeks, and the Carthaginians, the Romans, the Goths, and the Saracens.

In later times, it has generally shared the fate of Naples; but by the Treaty of Utrecht, it was given to the Duke of Savoy, who, however, was soon obliged, by the Quadruple Alliance, to return it to the Emperor, in exchange for Sardinia. The Spaniards seized this opportunity of renewing their claims, and sent a large armament, which had subdued the whole island, except Messina, which they were besieging, when Sir George Byng appeared with the British fleet.

The Spanish squadron, apprized of his approach, passed through the straits, and stood to the southward; Sir George pursued and brought it to action. Our fleet consisted of twenty-one sail of the line, carrying 1400 guns, the enemy's of eighteen, carrying 992 guns. Both sides fought bravely, but our superior numbers soon prevailed. Don Antonio de Casteneta, the Spanish Admiral, was taken prisoner, and only seven of his two-deckers escaped, of which the greater part were afterwards burnt at Messina, and one was lost in the Gulf of Tarento. Many of the frigates were also taken.

April 11th, 1718.

Six line of battle ships, and as many smaller men of war, which separated from the main body of the Spanish fleet, at the commencement of the action, were pursued by Commodore Walton, and every one taken or burnt; on which occasion

occasion he wrote this famous letter. " We have taken or destroyed all the " enemy's ships and vessels on the coast, " as per margin."

After this victory, Sir George Byng convoyed an army from the continent, and besieged the citadel of Messina, which the enemy's troops had now taken; and when the place was nearly reduced, a dispute arising among the allies on shore, about the Spanish men of war in the mole, Sir George, knowing that it is more our interest to reduce the navy of the rest of Europe, than to increase our own, caused batteries to be erected for shells and red-hot shot, and ended the contention, by destroying the cause.

The loss of their fleet, and many other disasters, obliged the Spaniards to accede to the Quadruple Alliance in 1720, and to relinquish their claim to Sicily

Sicily and Sardinia. But the Emperor having forfeited the protection of England, the Spaniards, about fifteen years after this treaty, made themselves masters of Sicily and Naples, as I have already related.

Messina was surrounded on the land side by a strong rampart, which, since the earthquake, has been entirely neglected. The Citadel is a regular square fort, with ravelins, counterguards, and a good covered way. It stands on that part of the neck of land which forms the mole, where this neck joins the island, and is kept in excellent condition; yet notwithstanding its artificial strength, it is of little use but as a place of arms, since an enemy having possession of the town, may destroy every vessel under its guns; but two other strong castles secure the shipping from any insult from the sea.

The

The neighbourhood is excessively fertile and populous, and we find the people very civil; but in the interior country, I am told they are rather savage.

LETTER XIII.

TO CAPTAIN SMITH.

Modon, October 19.

MY DEAR FRIEND,

WE are, at laſt, arrived on the confines of Greece, a venerable name, now almoſt loſt in that of Turkey in Europe, and its former ſplendour ſo entirely reverſed, that I am particularly fortunate in finding a conveyance for a letter. Here are no poſts in this neglected country, and the people once ſo accompliſhed, are in utter ignorance of what paſſes in the world, except from the vague reports they get from veſſels, which now and then put in here. And this, alas! is the unhappy fate of all the ſouth and eaſtern coaſt of Greece.

But

But before I say any thing more of this place, I must carry you back to Messina, and give you some account of our voyage.

Thursday, October 9th.

We left Messina at eleven o'clock this morning, and at twelve passed Reggio on the coast of Calabria. The country appears extremely barren, but is full of inhabitants and small towns.

Just before midnight, when all below were locked in sleep, and even those upon deck had scarce strength to resist the drowsy langour brought on by four hours duty; in this silent moment, when superstition, ever powerful in the mind of the sailor, gains new force from the surrounding gloom, the watch were rouzed with terror and astonishment, by a sudden illumination of the whole atmosphere. Their eyes, instantly turned to Heaven, were scarce reverted, when

every

every part of the ship appeared in a blaze, and continued so for many seconds.

Struck by so awful a sight, in the dead of the night, a general silence prevailed, and many, unable to divine the cause of so sudden, and so tremendous an apparition, thought the last day was approaching. Their fears were still increased by observing through the sails, an immense ball of fire floating in the air a-head of the ship; but they were, at length, relieved by its falling into the sea.

The account our friends gave us the next morning, led us into a dissertation on fireballs, which philosophers say are produced by an exceeding great power of electricity, gradually accumulated, until the resistance of the atmosphere being no longer able to sustain it, it drops down slowly, and in no particular direction,

rection, not being drawn by any substance which would attract this electric matter, in the shape of common lightning.

October 10th.

Sunset. A westerly breeze has carried us past Cape Spartevento, and we are now just an hundred miles from the coast of Sicily. Mount Ætna is still in sight, and the sun setting directly behind it, forms one of those heavenly scenes, which at once affects us with the beautiful and sublime. Notwithstanding our very great distance, the mountain is so many degrees above the horizon, that would day-light continue, we should see it twenty miles farther. How great does nature appear in these wonderful works!

October 11th.

Lat. 37° 36'. In the last twenty-four hours we have run an hundred and forty-

forty-three miles, and are so far across the Adriatic, or Gulph of Venice, as to have land in sight a-head. This breeze is almost the only fair one we have had since we left Gibraltar, and it is now growing calm.

October 12th.

Sunset. We are now between Zante and Cephalonia, with the Morea in front. The part of the islands near us are very rocky and barren, with no verdure except from some scattered olive trees, and brushwood; but the more distant part of Cephalonia appears well cultivated.

Sunday, October 14th.

We lay to all the night before last, and yesterday morning anchored in the harbour of Zante. Lat. 37°. 50′. Long. 21°. 15′. east.

The nearest part of this island is nine miles from Cephalonia, and the same distance from the Morea, and an hundred leagues from Messina. It is above seventy miles in circumference; contains forty thousand souls, and carries on a very considerable trade in dried fruits, particularly currants, so called from a corruption of Corinth, from whence the vines were originally imported.

On the hill above the town there is a fort, very advantageously situated, but much out of repair. It is subject to the Venetians, who have now a ship of the line and three frigates in the harbour. The senior Captain very civilly informed us, that, from his great respect for the English, he would be happy to salute us, if we would return gun for gun; to which we readily consented.

By orders from Venice, the Governor at this juncture, imposes a quarantine of seven days on all vessels, even from his own nearest ports; and therefore, not being allowed to land here, we are going to a less frequented part of the island, where the quarantine is not enforced.

October 15th.

We got under way yesterday evening, and the wind not permitting us to continue our voyage, we stood to the north-east towards Patras, at the mouth of the Gulf of Lepanto; but the wind changing, we put about at twelve this morning, just as we got in sight of its entrance, near the spot on which Don John of Austria obtained the celebrated victory over the Turkish fleet in the year 1571.

In this cruize we have had a view of Ithaca, in which we were told at Zante, the foundation of Ulysses' Palace is still to be traced. His island is now called

called Little Cephalonia, is about twenty miles long, appears very barren, but is said to be well peopled, though with a very vile race. Zante and the greater Cephalonia alfo belonged to Ulyffes, and are both defcribed by the ancients, as being remarkably fertile. The latter is by much the largeft, the former the moft productive.

A little to the north of Ithaca, in the Ifland of St. Mauro, is the famous Promontory of Leucate, the Lover's Leap, celebrated by the Spectator, is his beautiful panegyric on the tender Sappho. Even Venus herfelf is faid to have been led there by Apollo, to be cured of her paffion for Adonis.

October 16th.

Wind again contrary. Tacking off Zante, to get into a fmall bay, where there is a curious fpring, from which a great quantity of tar oozes; but not being able to gain the anchorage before sunset, and the wind becoming fair for our course, we stood to the south, and in the night passed the Strophades, a set of small low islands, where Æneas was attacked by the Harpies.

It was not without regret that I passed by Zante, without landing there. It was the only place in the Venetian territories we had any chance of visiting, and I wished much to see the effect of a Government, in which Despotism, in the form of a Republic, makes her votaries believe that Tyranny is Liberty. But by what I could learn from the traders, and a few other people, to whom I had an opportunity of speaking, the police is really shocking.

The Governors are generally needy men, but, by accepting fines as a remission for murder, they are soon enriched, perhaps by the ruin of the widow

dow and the orphan.—Is your hufband affaffinated—your father murdered? Dry up your tears—your Governor is three guineas richer. Do you remonftrate? For three guineas more you may let loofe all the demons of revenge.

Thus one murder produces another; whole families are involved in deftruction, or at beft live in perpetual alarms; juftice never interferes, and fociety is of courfe deftroyed.

Whilft reflections of this kind diftrefs the Philanthrope who vifits Zante, the naturalift finds the tar fpring an object well worthy his curiofity. The trade of the ifland is alfo a fubject on which I fhould like to be better informed. On an average, the annual produce in currants is ten million pounds weight. Almoft the whole of which, befides nearly the fame quantity brought from Cephalonia, and the adjacent parts of the Morea, are taken by the English, who load thirty vessels every year.

This trade, however, seems to be a very losing one to us, since our productions have no sale at Zante, and the tin, lead, alum, and a few other articles which we carry to Venice, bear no proportion in value to the fruit we bring home.

It is true, our revenue is considerably increased by a duty of twenty-three pounds sterling on every ton of currants, which is one half as much again as the prime cost, the common price at Zante being fifteen guineas. But this tax is raised upon ourselves, and does not check the importation of this foreign commodity, since we consume three-fourths of what the island yields. It might, therefore, as well be levied on some of our own productions, as on our hereditary plumb-pudding.

October

October 17th.

Having paffed two little forts, called the Navarins, at noon we anchored off Modon, Lat. 37°, Long. 15° 45', diftant from Gibraltar near fourteen hundred miles. And now, having brought the fhip to an anchor, I fhall proceed with the obfervations I introduced at the commencement of this letter.

Modon is a fmall Turkifh town, on the fouth-weft corner of the Morea, which you recollect is the Peloponnefus of the Ancients, and almoft an ifland, being feparated from the reft of Greece by the gulph of Lepanto, and only joined to it by the narrow ifthmus of Corinth. After the Greek and Roman ages, it was conquered by the Turks, and afterwards by the Venetians, to whom the former ceded it by the Treaty of Carlowitz, but retook it in 1715, and have maintained it ever fince, notwithftanding that, during their laft war, Modon was taken by by the Russians, who were immediately joined by the Greeks; but the Turks sending a large army thither, Count Orlow and his troops were obliged to abandon their associates to the fury of their enemies, who massacred fifteen thousand of them.

This is the Turkish method of terminating a rebellion, which they say is only to be done by destroying the seeds: but, to palliate their inhumanity, they allege, that, whenever the Greeks have gained any advantage, they have been still more barbarous; that they have spared neither age nor sex; but that, after being guilty of every other brutality to the women, so sacred among Mahometans, not satisfied with slaying them, they have even carried their revenge so far as to expose their naked corpses to be devoured by dogs and birds of prey.

Heaven

Heaven forbid that such cruel barbarity should exist. But I cannot pretend to give you a just account of the manners and dispositions of these two people on so slight an acquaintance, especially as the light in which they represent each other, is very different from that in which they appear to us.

Nestor's kingdom was in this district. I have found no antiquities worthy notice; and time does not permit me to take a journey in search of Pylos.

A small castle projects into the sea off Modon; and the town has walls round it; but they are much out of repair. The Governor lives in a wretched hovel, which refuses admittance neither to the wind nor to the rain. He is civil enough, and all his people seem glad to see us.

The harbour is formed by a set of little islands, which lie off the town, at
some

some miles distance; the most western is the famous Spactaria, the taking of which is one of the most noted events in the Peloponnesian war. It is now called the Isle of Wisdom; but for what reason I cannot guess, as it is totally uninhabited, and produces nothing but brushwood.

The passages between the different islands make this a charming port for cruizers, since they can be confined neither by wind nor by an enemy. Captain Moore, of the Fame privateer, often put in here during the war, and has impressed the people with very favorable ideas of the English.

LETTER XIV.

TO CAPTAIN SMITH.

Smyrna, November 14th.

MY DEAR FRIEND,

CONVINCED that you will be happy to hear of our arrival in Afia, I take advantage of the firft courier to fend you a letter.

Independent of the fatisfaction of being in a region fo noted in hiftory, and of traverfing fcenes which one has fo often contemplated in the page of antiquity, we have the happinefs of finding a fociety we did not expect in this loft country—a foil where the iron hand of Defpotifm checks every generous fentiment in the vanquifhed Greek, and where

where the conqueror Turk, proud in his ignorance, scorns the refinements of more enlightened people, and looks down with insolence or contempt on every nation but his own. He has, however, many good qualities; and his true character, I perceive, is not easily delineated. I shall consider him attentively, and from time to time send you those traits I discover. In the mean while, I will conclude this letter with my Journal from our leaving Modon to our arrival at this city.

Saturday, October 20th.

At eight o'clock this morning, we left Modon, and, at three in the afternoon, were opposite Cape Matapan. The country appears barren; but there are several villages in sight.

In the night, we entered the Archipelago, or Ægean Sea, by passing between Cytherea (the Island of Venus, now called Serigo)

Serigo) and Cape Angelo, the south-east point of the Morea.

This neighbourhood is inhabited by a nest of pirates, who call themselves the real descendants of the Lacedemonians, and, though subject to the Turks, acknowlege no law.

In calm weather, they come off in large boats, and plunder every vessel that passes, but seldom seize on any ship, or even molest the people, provided they allow them to take all they want.

It is very remarkable, that, although the French have always a force in these seas, their vessels are more frequently plundered than those of any other nation; and there are very few instances of ours being insulted, notwithstanding the Greeks so seldom see a British man of war.

But,

But, for fear of accidents, we shortened sail, to convoy the *Adventure*, of Plymouth, which we had just overtaken.

The three Sclavonians who seized the *Duchess of Tuscany*, bound from Gibraltar, meant to have brought her here, but being obliged to put into Zante, they were discovered and executed.

Sunday, October 21st.

Becalmed in the scene of Falconer's Shipwreck, Crete just discernible on our right, Falcanero on our left, and Milo a-head. Lat. 36° 38′.

At dusk the wind sprang up, with violent squalls, accompanied by thunder and lightning, and soon burst forth in a furious storm.

We were now in a most unpleasant situation, Milo was become a dangerous lee

lee fhore. It was no comfort to know that there was an excellent harbour a few miles to leeward. Darknefs prevented our feeing the entrance to it.

We were, therefore, obliged to haul clofe to the wind, and by fkill, attention, and perfeverance, happily weathered the moft windward point of the ifland.

The wind then abated, and the fea became lefs violent; but the next morning the ftorm was fuddenly renewed, and we were affailed more furioufly than ever; but as day-light came to our affiftance, we made the beft of our way towards the harbour, and a pilot getting on board, we were fafe at an anchor before twelve o'clock.

Some centuries before Chrift, Milo was a flourifhing Republic, but having refufed its affiftance to Greece, when it

was

was invaded by the Persians, the Athenians, having defeated the Barbarians, attacked the Miliotes, and after several repulses, at last entirely overthrew them, and as a punishment, all the men who escaped the sword, were carried into Attica. But at the close of the Peloponnesian war, the Athenians being subdued by the Lacedemonians, Milo was restored to its liberty. It was afterwards taken by the Romans, and has ever since shared the fate of the Eastern Empire. And for some centuries the Greeks have been slaves in a country, from which they often carried their arms into that of their present Lords.

A. A. C. 404.

Whatever the Turk conquers, he immediately considers as his own, whether it be land, cattle, men, women, or children, and instantly appropriates it to his use, either by sale, exchange, or possession.

But

But as an act of grace, the Sultan grants the Greeks a temporary emancipation from year to year, for which they pay an annual capitation tax of seven shillings each person.

At the commencement of this century the island contained seventeen churches, and eleven chapels; and the whole space from the town to the harbour, which is near two miles, was laid out in beautiful gardens. But alas! how wretchedly is it altered, three-fourths of the towns are in ruins, and the inhabitants are daily decreasing. Of the gardens scarce a vestige is left; and the baths on the water side are now only a set of small, dirty caves. Eight or ten yards from the shore the hot spring, which supplied them, is seen boiling through the salt water, and the sand is, I think, still hotter than that of Baia. But perhaps I speak from the pain my
curiosity

curiosity cost me being more recent in my memory.

The women, so celebrated for their beauty, are now sallow, unhealthy, and disgustingly ugly; and render themselves still more hideous by their dress, which is a kind of loose jacket, with a white cotton petticoat, that scarcely covers two thirds of their thighs, barely meeting the stocking above the knee. Their hind hair hangs down the back in a number of plaits; that on the fore part of the head is combed down each side of the face, and terminated by a small, stiff curl, which is even with the lower part of the cheek.

All the inhabitants are Greeks; for the Turks are not fond of trusting themselves in the small islands; but every summer the Captain Bashaw goes round with a squadron to keep them in subjection, and to collect the revenue.

When

When the Ruffians made themfelves mafters of the Archipelago, during the late war, many of the iflands declared in their favour; but being abandoned at the peace, they were fo feverely mulcted by the Grand Signior, that our pilot tells me, they are determined to remain perfectly quiet. But as the Turks do not think them worth a garrifon, and will not truft them with arms and ammunition, all thofe which the Ruffians may choofe to invade, will be obliged to fubmit.

The two points which form the entrance of the harbour, croffing each other, render it imperceptible until you are clofe to it. Thus, while you are perfectly fecure within it, you find great difficulty in getting out, particularly in a northerly wind. And as no trade is carried on, except a little in corn and falt, Milo would fcarce ever be vifited, were it not that being the firft ifland one makes in the Archipelago, the pilots have chofen it for their refidence. They live in a little town on the top of a high rock, which, from its fituation and appearance, is called *The Caftle*.

Partridges abound in this ifland, and are fo cheap, that you may buy one for a charge of powder only. The peafants get them by ftanding behind a portable fcreen, with a fmall aperture in the center, in which they place the muzzle of their piece, and then draw the partridge by a call. When a fufficient number are collected, they fire among them, and generally kill from four to feven at a fhot. But even this method of getting them is fo expenfive, from the fcarcity of ammunition, that the people can never afford to fhoot them, but when there are gentlemen in the ifland, from whom they can beg a little powder and fhot.

Several

Several of us have killed four or five in an afternoon walk, putting them up ourfelves, without even the affiftance of a dog.

Thurfday, October 25th.

At day-break we got under way, with a light breeze, and at midnight anchored at Paros, another of the Greek iflands, and which is in a much better ftate than Milo. The men look more healthy, and the women not fo ugly.

The water here is excellent; and as that we got at Meffina has been complained of, as being too hard to make proper peafe-foup for the people, all the cafks are ordered to be emptied and refilled.

Whilft its marble quarries continued to be worked, Paros was one of the moft flourifhing of the Cyclades; but on the decline of the Eaftern Empire,

they

they were entirely neglected, and are now converted into caves, in which the shepherds shelter their flocks. We have been in several of these subterraneous folds, which put me much in mind of Homer's description of Polyphemus. The common walls are almost entirely composed of marble; and in examining a very small part of one, we found several pieces of cornice, and *basso relievo*.

Several fine blocks of marble—fragments of columns, are lying close to the water's edge, and seem to have been brought there by travellers, who for want of a proper purchase to get them on board, have not been able to carry them farther.

After the battle of Marathon, Miltiades was sent to lay Paros under contribution, on account of its joining the Persians; but the inhabitants made so resolute

resolute a defence, that all the efforts of that excellent General were unable to reduce them; and, at length, having loft a number of his men, and being himself wounded, Miltiades, hearing that the Persians were making preparations for a second invasion, returned to Athens, where his ungrateful countrymen, forgetful of his eminent services, sentenced him to pay the expences of the expedition; and being unable to raise this fine, the Great Deliverer of Greece was thrown into prison; and, to the eternal infamy of the Athenians, he died of the wounds he had received in their service!

The Ruffians made this their grand arsenal; their powder magazines, and several other buildings, are still standing, and the island is confiderably indebted to them for improving the convenience for water, and for the trade which the

cafh

cash they expended, introduced among the inhabitants.

Delos is about five leagues off, Naxos two, and Antiparos about the same distance. In the last there is a cavern, which is reckoned one of the greatest wonders of the Archipelago; but as a natural curiosity, it is by no means equal to Saint Michael's Cave at Gibraltar. A multitude of names are cut near the entrance. Lady Craven's is among the latest.

Tuesday, October 30th.

Sailed from Paros, with an intention of visiting Delos in our way to Smyrna, but the wind changing, we stood to the north-west, profiting by this opportunity, to supply the ship with wood.

Wednesday, October 31st.

Anchored between the Island of Longa and the Coast of Immortal Attica. But my heart bleeds whilft I furvey the fad change it has undergone. In vain do I fearch for the defcendants of thofe ruftic patriots, whofe valour enabled Miltiades and Themiftocles to overthrow the Perfian hoft by fea and land, or for thofe well cultivated fields, where art concealed the frugality of nature. Alas! far as the beft glafs can reach, no fign of a dwelling can be feen; and the country, for want of inhabitants, lies entirely neglected.

After almoft defpairing of meeting a human being, I one day fell in with two men grazing a confiderable number of horfes, which I imagined was a nurfery for the Turkifh Cavalry; but on mentioning this to the Greeks who attended them, they anfwered no; that the only ufe they were of was to tread out the corn in fummer; in return for which they grazed them from place to place in winter. I alfo found a fmall chapel,

not

not bigger than an hermitage, to which the people from the interior country, on particular occasions, resort. Part of the neighbourhood is covered with wood, which any one may take who chooses to cut it. Longa, the once celebrated Island of Helen, is entirely depopulated, and produces nothing. Our pilot calls this Port Maundré. It has the same advantage I remarked at Modon, a passage at each end of the island.

If you can believe that I am within a day's journey of Athens, how will you envy my being so near the mother of the arts and sciences, and what will you say when I tell you that I did not go there. But be assured it was not through want of exertion; but from the impracticability of getting there by land in these hostile times. But whilst the people were wooding, I went in a boat to the Promontory of Sunium, to see the remains of the Temple of Minerva,

which

which I take to be one of the moſt ancient remaining in Greece. If we may credit Homer, it was cotemporary with Troy; for in the third book of the Odyſſey, Neſtor, after relating the ſeduction of Clytemneſtra, paſſing to the return of the Greeks, ſays,

> " But when to Sunium's ſacred point we came,
> " Crown'd with the Temple of the Athenian Dame,
> " Atrides Pilot, Phrontes, there expired, &c."

In ſome ground lately opened I found a human ſcull, and ſome other burnt bones. What antiquarian will object to their being thoſe of this ill-fated pilot?

A conſiderable part of the architrave of the Temple is ſtill ſtanding, ſupported by fifteen columns, nine of which are in a row, each nineteen feet high, and near eleven in circumference. The whole edifice was of Parian marble. Vaſt quantities of fragments and broken columns are

are lying all around, and the Temple is still a beautiful, and a venerable object, on whatever side you approach the Promontory.

November 5th.

Got under way at day-light, and having passed the south point of Negropont (the ancient Euboea) and Andros, were opposite the center of the Island of Teno at twelve o'clock the next day. It seems populous and well cultivated. Lat. 37° 33'. Paros, Delos, and several other islands in sight.

November 7th.

We were within a few leagues of Scio at day-break, and being driven to the southward, had a distant view of Samos, the birth place of Juno. We were employed all this and the next day in working to windward, between the continent of Asia Minor and the Island of Scio, famous for producing the nectar of the ancients,

ancients, and for the beauty of its women. The ladies, I am told, are as charming as ever, but the wine has loft its lufcious qualities. The town is large and ftraggling; it feems to have fome works, but they are in a very forry condition. The road is quite open. Before we reached the town, we paffed the bay of Chifemé, on the Afiatic fhore, where the Turkifh fleet was deftroyed by the Ruffians.

Friday, Nov. 9th, 1787.

A light breeze fprang up fair late laft night, with which we entered the Gulf of Smyrna, and early this afternoon anchored off the town.

LETTER XV.

TO CAPTAIN SMITH.

Smyrna, November 29th.

MY DEAR FRIEND,

SMYRNA is the only ancient town of Asia Minor, that continues to thrive. It flourished many centuries before Christ, but was almost destroyed by an earthquake in the reign of Mark Anthony, and has never since recovered its former splendour. For although its advantageous situation for trade soon drew new inhabitants, yet, to lessen the effect of a similar catastrophe, the houses are all very low. The streets are in general dirty, narrow, and ill-paved, for the natives never study regularity in the scite of their buildings, and the Europeans, crowding

crowding to the water fide, found no room to fpare for ornament.

The French have the moft numerous factory. The Englifh are next in number of houfes, but the Dutch exceed us in fhipping. The Venetian and Ragufee veffels are very numerous, but they are feldom more than carriers.

The great advantage England derives from the trade to this country is, that the commodities we bring here are home-wrought, whilft the filk, cotton, and mohair, with which we are repaid, are raw articles, that are afterwards manufactured by ourfelves, find work for our people, and are then exported to different parts of the world, and fome of them even brought back here.

Befides filk and cotton, we take fruit and drugs, fome of which are alfo re-exported; but I am forry to find, that
though

though our Levant trade is more flourishing than it has been for many years paſt, yet its riſe is conſiderably checked by our own laws, and by the want of a regular Lazaretto in England.

If there is the leaſt ſuſpicion of the plague being at Smyrna, no veſſel, even of our own nation, is permitted to diſcharge her cargo in Britain, previous to her having performed a quarantine in ſome other part of Europe; for our Lazarettos do not admit veſſels from infected ports. But ſince our manufactories muſt be ſupplied with ſilk and cotton, our merchants are obliged to employ the Dutch, who land their goods in a Lazaretto in Holland, and after a ſhort quarantine performed there, ſend them over to us. Thus do we ſuffer foreigners to deprive our ſeamen of employment, and our country of its juſt profits.

The

The cause that produces this prejudice to our Levant Company, is our dread of the plague. But are we more likely to be infected by this distemper than the Dutch? Or is England less able than Holland to set apart a small place for a regular Lazaretto? There are innumerable spots in our island which might be inclosed for this purpose, where goods from infected places might be properly aired, and afterwards introduced with more safety by our own subjects, than we at present receive them from the Dutch.

A person who has not been in the Levant, cannot conceive the inconvenience and distress arising to our nation, from this want of a Lazaretto. The enterprising spirit of the English leads them every where in search of employment. A vessel arrives at Smyrna—she gets a cargo, and the last day of her loading perhaps the plague appears on shore.

shore. What is she to do? She cannot sail for England—she must either submit to a ruinous loss, unload immediately, and fly to another port in quest of a freight, or go to one of the Lazarettos of Italy, France, or Malta, there perform a quarantine, land and reship her cargo; and after having, to the prejudice of the nation, laid out a considerable sum in a foreign port, she arrives at Stangate Creek; where, though the ship perhaps is not long detained, the cargo is put into one of the hulks, and aired with greater care and length of time, than the cotton has been which we receive without any apprehension from Holland *.

That

---

* The Author since his return to England, has been at Stangate Creek, where he found that cotton, and other enumerated goods brought over from Holland, now undergo a similar process to those, which, after having performed a quarantine in a foreign Lazaretto, are brought home by the English.

That precautions are necessary nobody will deny; but why should we shackle our own people more than the Dutch? Or why should we be more afraid of allowing goods from an infected place to be landed in one of the many waste spots of Kent, Essex, Devonshire, or Cornwall, than foreigners are of receiving them at the very gates of their capital cities. I shall write you a long letter on this subject, when I have gained more experience in the nature of the plague, which I can already assure you is by no means so dangerous a distemper as Europeans imagine it.

The factory have great hopes that the generous Philanthrope, who lately visited Asia, will interest himself in their favour. This amiable patriot knows that

English. But still the inconvenience to our own people is not lessened, nor ever will, till we have a complete Lazaretto of our own.

the navy is the bulwark of Britain, and that whatever tends to decreaſe the number of our ſeamen, tends to diminiſh the ſtrength of our country; a truth ſo intereſting to an Engliſhman, that I hope to God the accounts I hear of a moſt alarming decreaſe in our Greenlandmen are much exaggerated. A proper Lazaretto in England, by increaſing our ſhipping in the Levant, would afford a ſuſtenance to many of thoſe invaluable ſubjects, whom a perhaps too rigid public œconomy has bereft of bread.

There are many inconveniencies attending a correſpondence between this country and Europe. The poſt ſets out and arrives but twice a month. It goes through Conſtantinople and Vienna, and unleſs letters to and from England are taken up, and paid for at each of thoſe places, they will never reach their deſtination. The want of a more regular communication muft be fenfibly felt in a place of fo much trade.

We found near one hundred fail of merchantmen in the bay, every one of whom faluted us; for, to raife the European Powers in the eyes of the Turks, it is the cuftom at Smyrna to falute every man of war that enters the port. The fame ceremony was performed on our going on fhore the next day; and, as foon as we landed at Mr. Hayes', we were waited upon by the Confuls and Factories of the different nations, who have given us the moft flattering reception. Scarce an evening paffes without a ball or a concert, or fome other party, for our amufement: but I am much furprifed at the exceffive dread in which the Chriftians live of their fellow fubjects, the Mahometans. They dwell in feparate diftricts, and are as fearful of going promifcuoufly among them, as into a

den

den of wild beasts. The Turks have, indeed, a lordly, imperious air, which I suppose they acquire from the abject manner of the Greeks, who, being a conquered people, are always suspected of rebellious intentions, and almost extirpated on the least appearance of an insurrection; which obliges them to crouch so much to the conquerors, that they imagine all other Christians equally dastardly, and hold us in the same light as we do the Jews—a mean, money-making, unbelieving sect: but I am convinced, that if we went more among them, we should hear of fewer insults. I was so confident of this, that, without mentioning my intentions, I set out, and, after walking round the Turkish town, struck down through its very center, without meeting any interruption, except from one man, who, pointing at me, called out *Bah!* and two or three boys, who threw stones, but who were immediately called in by their father.

father. I doubt whether a foreigner, in a ſtrange dreſs, would paſs through London with ſo little moleſtation.

Neverthelefs, like the Jews in England, there have been inſtances here of the Chriſtians being moſt inhumanly maſſacred; but this has never happened but after ſome ſignal diſaſter to the Turks, to which they ſuppoſed they had contributed; ſuch as the deſtruction of their fleet in the Chifemé, which they knew the Ruſſians could not have effected without the aſſiſtance of other powers; and the rabble make very little diſtinction of nations, confounding all Europeans together, under the appellation of Franks.

The poor Greeks complain much of their cruelty and oppreſſion; but, in points of honour, our merchants tell me no people are ſtricter than the Turks. In other reſpects, the reports they give of their laws and cuftoms, vary fo much, that it is impoffible for a ftranger, as I am, and ignorant of the language of the country, to fend you a more perfect account.

LETTER XVI.

TO CAPTAIN SMITH.

Smyrna, December 31st.

MY DEAR FRIEND,

THE Empress of Russia's late journey to the Crimea, and the confederacy formed there by her Majesty and the Emperor of Germany, have given the late stroke to those reiterated provocations which would, long ere this, have excited to arms a people less irascible than the Turks: but, however inclined the nation at large might be to resent the insults of the Russians, and the frequent infringements of the Treaty of Cainardgie, yet their fiery spirit was kept in awe by the pacific disposition of the reigning Sultan.

Abdoul

Abdoul Hamet is a Prince of a humane and virtuous character; and, although the peace of 1774 was forced upon his country, he determined moſt religiouſly to adhere to the conditions it impoſed.

At the time this treaty was concluded, the Porte was in a moſt deplorable ſtate, to which it was in a great meaſure reduced by the unprecedented ſupport the Engliſh afforded to the ambitious views of the Court of Peterſburg, againſt a nation with whom we were at peace.

The Spaniards were well inclined to prevent the Ruſſian fleet entering the Mediterranean; but their objections were quaſhed at once by the interference of ſo brilliant a Power as England: a Power whoſe all-conquering force the Court of Spain had ſo recently felt, in the repeated victories of the immortal Chatham, which had obliged her to ſupplicate peace at the feet of our glorious Sovereign.

A George,

A George, and a Chatham, are names which the patriotic Englishman could for ever dwell upon; but both the politics of the one, and the virtues of the other, are too exalted to be extended by a panegyric from my humble pen. To return, then, to the Turks, and to a time when, I am sorry to say, our prejudice in favor of Russia, made us adopt a line of conduct in a high degree contrary to our own interest: The terror of the English having compelled the Spaniards to suffer the Russians to enter the Mediterranean, our port at Mahon immediately received them with open arms. Here they were not only supplied with every refreshment, but our hospitals, nay, even our arsenals, were opened to them, and every encouragement was given to our officers and seamen, to enter into their service.

Thus supplied and equipped, the Russian fleet sailed for the Archipelago, and

and gave battle to the Turks. Victory (as may naturally be suppofed, from the fuperior abilities and nautical experience of Commodore Elphinftone and the Britifh officers) declared for the Ruffians.

The Ottoman fleet retired to the Bay of Chifemé; and the Mofcovites, unaccuftomed to naval exertions, were not difpofed to purfue their advantage. It was with the utmoft difficulty that Commodore Elphinftone could perfuade them to follow the enemy, and attack him in port: but at length, by threats and entreaties, having ftimulated them to this enterprize, he led them to the Chifemé the enfuing night. The Turks, aftonifhed at the unexpected attack, were inftantly panic-ftruck, and, without any fhew of defence, abandoned and fet fire to their fhips.

Thus did an Englifhman give a fatal blow to the Turkifh empire—a blow from

from which I much doubt whether the Porte will ever recover.

Commodore Elphinstone instantly pushed for the Dardanelles, and, by guarding the entrance of those straits, cut off all communication by sea between Constantinople and the southern provinces. The capital was streightened for provisions; Egypt revolted, and most of the Greek islands joined the Russians.

These were the first consequences of the disaster at Chisemé; and every day brought on others still more distressing to the Porte.

The Russian fleet, now unopposed, was enabled to attack every part of the Turkish coast in the Adriatic, the Archipelago, and the Mediterranean; and, although the troops they had on board were but few, yet, from the facility with
which

which they were transported from place to place, the Turks were obliged to detach a very large part of their grand army to oppose their different attacks.

But this was not all. Many of the soldiers employed to the north, were volunteers from the southern provinces, who, hearing that their own homes were attacked, deserted in large corps. These desertions, and the detachments sent to the south, weakened and discouraged the northern army so much, that the Russians gained repeated victories, and at last compelled the Porte to sue for peace.

The Treaty of Cainardgie was highly humiliating in itself, and was rendered still more so by the haughty manner of the Russians, which seemed entirely calculated to provoke the Turks to hostilities, in which they have at last succeeded.

Monsieur

Monsieur Bulgakow, the Russian Envoy, who had been sent for by the Empress, to assist at the conferences between her Majesty and the Emperor of Germany, and probably to give the Confederate Powers information of the disposition, and the measures most likely to be pursued by the Porte, had no sooner returned to Constantinople, than the Turkish Ministry, convinced of the oppressive and aspiring views of the Court of Petersburgh, made the Envoy a formal representation of the many causes of complaint his Court had given to the Porte.

This representation was followed by a second; but the Envoy, in conformity, I suppose, to the plan agreed upon at Cherson, gave no manner of satisfaction, and the hostile views of his Court becoming every day more notorious, the Porte summoned him to a conference on the 16th of August, and there demanded

manded a categorical explanation of the intentions of the Emprefs towards the Turks.

M. Bulgakow's anfwers appearing vague and unfatisfactory, the Divan determined to have recourfe to arms, and in conformity to the Turkifh cuftom on fuch occafions, the Envoy, with part of his fuite and attendants, were fent to the Seven Towers, where, though ftate prifoners, they have every indulgence but liberty. And fuch is the pacific difpofition of the Sultan, that he declares his only motive in going to war, is to inforce the conditions impofed by the Treaty of Cainardgie—a treaty, which, though the moft difadvantageous the Turks ever figned, he declares himfelf ftill ready to renew.

The manifefto publifhed by the Porte ftates, that ever fince the year 1774, the Court of Ruffia has been conftantly infringing

infringing the Treaty of Cainardgie, and disturbing the harmony which that treaty was intended to secure. That she has even seized on the Crimea, and raised up Prince Heraclius, who was an acknowleged vassal of the Porte. That not content with endeavouring to drive the Oczakowians from their own salt-pans, and many other attacks, she proceeded so far as to order her Envoy to make a demand of several dangerous and humiliating concessions from the Porte, and to threaten, that in case of a refusal, Prince Potemkin, with 70,000 men, had orders to advance to the frontiers. That since the Porte could not with any safety agree to these conditions, she was obliged to declare war. And submits her motives to the equity of her friends.

So vigorous a step was not immediately expected by the Empress; and had the Turks been in any degree prepared for the hostile measures they were compelled

compelled to adopt, the surprise in which they took the Russians, would probably have given them a decisive advantage.

The fact is, the Court of Petersburgh did not expect hostilities to commence before the ensuing spring, and the Turks never thought of them till M. Bulgakow's return from the Crimea. Thus both parties were equally surprised.

The season was too far advanced for the Grand Vizir to take the field. Those troops, however, that could be collected on the frontiers, immediately began to act, and in different recounters with the Russians, have been generally victorious.

No enterprize, however, of any moment has as yet been undertaken by the Turks, except an attack upon Kimbourn.

This fortrefs is fituated on the Ruffian fide of the Liman, or mouth of the Dnieper, exactly oppofite to Oczakow, and from its fituation is of the firft importance. The Porte therefore ordered an immediate attempt to carry it by a coup-de-main. A detachment from Oczakow was accordingly landed in the night of the 11th of October, and carried all before them till they arrived at the very fcarp of the fort; but by this time the Ruffians had recovered their furprife, and the Turks, from the nature of the enterprife, being unprepared to attempt a regular efcalade againft a garrifon whofe numbers they found were very little inferior to their own, were obliged to retreat.

The lofs on each fide was nearly equal, and on the part of the Ruffians, M. Souwarow and M. Reck, two generals of note, were both feverely wounded.

The Court of Peterſburgh, however, has great reaſon to rejoice at this eſcape, ſince had Kimbourn been carried, none of her veſſels could have entered the Liman till it was retaken, which probably would not have happened this year, and conſequently, ſhould the Porte even chooſe to act on the defenſive in the ſpring, the Ruſſians would ſtill be obliged to begin the enſuing campaign with a ſiege in their own country.

Count Romanzow, with an army, has entered Poliſh Ruſſia, but the ſeaſon was too far advanced for him to attempt any active operations. I have not heard any thing elſe of importance on the land ſide; but in the naval line, fortune has ſtruck a capital blow in favor of the Turks.

The little fleet the Empreſs had, with great difficulty, collected on the Black Sea has been entirely diſperſed and diſmaſted, and a line of battle ſhip, of
ſixty-

sixty-four guns, commanded by Captain Teesdale, to avoid being wrecked, was obliged to push for Constantinople, and give herself up to the Turks.

As she is very little damaged, she will sail in the spring, under the banners of the Porte. The Russians were before very inferior to the Turks on the Black Sea; and the loss of one ship to them making a difference of two in favor of their enemies, renders their inequality still more desperate.

The Turks having no idea of prisoners on parole, the Russian Captain is sent to associate with the Envoy in the Castle of the Seven Towers. The rest of the ship's company are disposed of in the Bagnio.

Notwithstanding our impolitic ill usage, so fatal to the Turks during the last Russian war, I think we are the favorite nation of such of them as are at all acquainted with the different powers of Europe: I say, impolitic ill usage, because, depend upon it, the very extensive Empire of Turkey will never be in hands so beneficial to England, as whilst it remains in those of its present possessors.

The Turks, happily for us, are not a commercial people, notwithstanding their Empire has every advantage to induce them to become so. We cannot do without those valuable articles which their soil produces almost spontaneously; and the Turk, like the easy possessor of a very rich mine, allows us to enrich ourselves at our pleasure. Three per cent. duty equally on all exports and imports, is, with little exception, their only restriction to Europeans engaged in their trade.

Would the Empress be equally moderate, if in possession of this fertile region?

gion? Believe me she would not. As several of our manufactures could not be carried on without her productions, she would only give them on her own terms. Perhaps only in her own bottoms. All her politics would be directed to increase her trade and shipping, and consequently her naval force; and, thus inclined, with such a country, she would soon rise to a maritime power much beyond what the world has ever experienced. We have only to look to Tyre, to Rhodes, and many other places scarce bigger than specks on the map of Turkey, to conceive what a force might arise from this immense, this all producing Empire.

In its present state, Turkey, as I have already hinted, may be compared to a rich mine, to which the industrious from every nation have free access. In the hands of the Empress it would be like the barred treasure of an ambitious Lord, never to be opened but to be increased.

In this I do not mean to reflect on her Imperial Majesty, since, I fancy, every European power, in a similar situation, would act the same part. I only desire to evince that England will never derive such advantages from Turkey, as whilst it remains in the hands of the Ottomans, and consequently that it is our interest, as well as that of every other nation that does not expect a share in the partition of the Turkish Empire, to break the confederacy between the Empress of Russia and the Emperor of Germany, and check the progress of the two Imperial Courts. I mention the Emperor, because, though he has not yet declared war, it is very well known that he is bound, both by treaty and inclination, to assist the Russians.

The French Court very wisely, in the last war, supported the Porte; but from the indifference with which she now beholds the threatened ruin of a power

with

with whom she trades to so much advantage, a rumour gains ground that she has been brought over to the ambitious views of the Imperial Courts, by the promise, that should their designs succeed, Egypt and the Island of Candia shall be given to France.

Should this ever happen, England may bid adieu to the trade of the Levant, and, in a short time, by the easy communication the French will establish with the East-Indies, by the way of the Isthmus of Suez, they will give a fatal blow to our India trade also.

To prevent these schemes from succeeding, our first object is to countenance the Spaniards in opposing the entrance of the Russian fleet into the Mediterranean; since, if the Turks can bring their whole force to act towards the north, I do not think, now that their fleet has such a decided superiority

on

on the Black Sea, that they have much to fear in the prefent ftate of Europe. The King of Sweden, were he countenanced, is well difpofed to take an open part in their favour; and this countenance the King of Pruffia will undoubtedly afford him.

As to Europe's having any thing to dread from the Turks extending their conqueft, the idea is abfurd. Their Empire is already larger than they well can keep in order; and, from the nature of their government, the more they extend it, the more will it be weakened. Their army may make irruptions, but muft foon return to its proper bounds.

They do not, like the Romans, incorporate the vanquifhed with the conquerors, fo as, in time, to become one people, and to increafe in numbers as they increafe in territory. On the
contrary

contrary, the farther the Turk advances in Europe, the more he augments the number of his rebellious fubjects, and by difperfing, he weakens his own.

Conftantinople excluded, the Grand Signior's fubjects in Europe are computed at eight Greeks to one Turk. Totally different in language, manners, and religion, a natural antipathy is bred between them. The Turk fpurns the Greek as an impious daftard. The Greek, urged by revenge, is ever ripe for a revolt, and ready to join the firft invaders.

If we confider this ftriking circumftance, and the fuccefs of the Ruffians in the laft war, it may be imagined, that on the Emperor's taking the field, the Turks will very foon be driven out of Europe; and of this our factory here are in the higheft apprehenfion. But we muft at the fame time recollect, that it was England who gave force to Ruffia, in the manner I before related, and that this force, if it does not now oppofe her, will, at leaft, not operate in her favor.

Monfieur St. Felix arrived here lately with a fquadron of frigates and floops, eight in number. The Governor immediately fent to the French Conful to know the meaning of fo many men of war coming to this port. M. Amoreux anfwered, that they only came in for refrefhments. Whether or not it was in confequence of this meffage, I cannot take upon me to affirm, but the majority of the French fquadron put to fea in the courfe of the two following days. This, I think, confirms that a jealoufy of France exifts in the minds of the Turks.

LETTER XVII.

TO CAPTAIN SMITH.

Smyrna, January 15th, 1788.

MY DEAR FRIEND,

TO gain some little knowledge of the interior country, and, at the same time, to pay a compliment to St. Paul, we took a journey by land to Ephesus, the inhabitants of which, you may remember, were honoured with an Epistle from him, and with having his son Timothy for a Bishop. It is barely forty miles from hence; but the Turks never going beyond a foot pace in travelling, we made it a journey of two days. We had six horses for ourselves, and as many for our guides, janizary, and servants. We were obliged to carry

carry all our provisions with us, even bread. Water we found in abundance; and such is the attention of the Turks to this valuable article of life, that we came to several excellent fountains when there was nothing like an habitation to be seen. The greater part of the road is execrably bad; and the country, though in general fertile, is too thinly peopled to be much cultivated.

The few inhabitants we saw in the second day's journey were wretchedly poor. You recollect that this is the freezing month of January, and that the winter here, though short, is, for a few weeks, much more severe than one would expect in so southern a latitude.

Our road led us by a fountain, where, in this cold weather, some women were washing. None of them were completely clothed; and one poor girl had, for her only covering, a piece of an old blanket,

blanket, with two holes torn in the upper end of it, through which, inſtead of ſleeves, ſhe put her arms. It was too ſmall to cover her cheſt, too ſhort to reach below her waiſt; and it was with difficulty that, by holding the lower corners in her two hands, ſhe made them meet.

A young female, in an attire ſo little adapted to the tenderneſs of her ſex, and to the inclemency of the ſeaſon, moved one's very ſoul. I do not know that I touched the reins, and yet my horſe ſtopt with his head towards her. My eye involuntarily fixed itſelf upon her; and, to the lateſt moment of my life, I ſhall never forget her figure. She is above the middle ſize, and her limbs did not ſeem formed for ſo expoſed a ſituation. The ſun had tanned her face; but her ſkin was ſmooth, and naturally delicate, and her features of that mould, that, had ſhe been born to a more happy lot,

lot, she might have been reckoned a perfect beauty.

It was impossible to behold such an object without emotion. My horse now advanced to her feet, and my friend approached her at the same moment. Each searched his pockets, and presented the little silver they contained. No hand could be spared to receive it. In our anxiety to relieve her distress, we had forgot the trial to which we had exposed her modesty. The blushing maid stood motionless; but, encouraged by the sympathy and charity marked in our approach, she ventured to raise her head.—Her eyes were turned towards us.—The tear of gratitude was swelling in them.—She gave but one glance.—Her face was instantly reverted to the ground.—She could not speak.

Such unexpected modesty, in so exposed a situation, filled me with astonishment

ment and veneration. How much did I wiſh to take her in my arms, and, by a kiſs of affection, to expreſs the ſympathy I bore in her diſtreſs. How did I execrate the parſimony that had prevented my having about me all the money I poſſeſſed.—How earneſtly did I wiſh to remove her to a more ſheltered fate, where her beauty and her modeſty might be better known and admired.

Led away by theſe inclinations, I was preparing to alight. The timid virgin drew back. By ſigns of reſpect, ſhe again raiſed her eyes. Charity was ſo forcibly petitioning in them, that the money which her figure at firſt ſight drew from my pocket, now dropt at her feet. The reins fell from my hand. My horſe inclined to the road. I would with joy have turned him back; but I recollected my inability to relieve her.— I am only a Soldier of Fortune, and ſubſiſt but by the bounty of my Sovereign:

reign: a bounty which, though much superior to what my humble services entitle me to expect, is, alas! too insufficient to support the appearance required from an Officer, and often compels the military Philanthrope to suppress every charitable emotion.

The road being but little frequented, the caravansera, or public inn, we stopped at the first night of our journey, was nothing but a large hovel, one end of which was appropriated to travellers, and the other, without any partition, to their cattle: but we were fortunate enough to be accommodated with a Greek hut, where, with the assistance of a good fire, we passed a tolerable night.

At Ephesus we were not so lucky. We were obliged to sleep promiscuously among the Turks, one or other of whom was smoking all night long. I observed that they eat very little, but that, after

every

every nap, they took a pipe, and a sip of coffee: I say, a sip; for the Turkish cups are scarce bigger than a walnut shell; but of these they drink an amazing number, and their coffee is always exceedingly strong.

We were heartily rejoiced when we returned to our old Greek hut on the road, but, to our great disappointment, found it possessed by a Turk. Luckily, he expressed a great desire to taste our beer; and we seized this opportunity to get rid of him, by desiring our janizary to invite him to partake of a bottle of it at the caravansera. A janizary's invitation is only a civil command; but we did not choose to make use of his authority until we could give the Turk a satisfactory compensation. Mahomet forbade the use of wine; but his followers do not conceive themselves to be prohibited the use of other fermented liquors. In general, they are very fond of porter

and

and beer of all kinds, drinking as much of it as they can get; and some of them, indeed, are not very scrupulous about wine.

After the Turk was gone, not dreaming of the danger that was hanging over us, we slept very comfortably for some hours; but, before day-light, we were roused by flakes of fire falling upon our bodies from the roof. No water being at hand, the whole hut was soon in a blaze, and, in a few minutes, burnt to the ground.

This unluckly accident was occasioned by our own fire, which heated the mud flue that served as a chimney, to such a degree, that it communicated to the thatched roof, which was half burnt through before we awoke. Very fortunately, none of us had taken off our clothes; for we carried no bedding, and nothing of the kind was to be got.

The

The Turks in the Caravanfera remained quiet fpectators of this cataftrophe. At the moment when we found that all our efforts to extinguifh the flames were ineffectual, my eye turning towards the Muffulmen, found them fmoking, and feemingly quite unconcerned.

Determined not to be outdone by them in coolnefs, I feated myfelf in the middle of them, and, being provided with the materials, inftantly began fhaving myfelf, to their no fmall aftonifhment, and the equal delight of the boys of our party, who have turned this anecdote into a pleafant ftory, which is my only reafon for mentioning it.

You of courfe recollect that the Temple of Diana at Ephefus, which was one of the wonders of the world, was deftroyed stroyed on the very day that Alexander was born, by a sacrilegious wretch, to render himself remembered by posterity. We found many ruins, and among the rest, a superb pile quite overturned, which we concluded was the remains of this celebrated temple. The columns were all broken. The most entire piece was forty-two feet in length, and eighteen in circumference. This and the rest of the columns, were every one hewn out of single blocks of marble; but notwithstanding the immense size and value of these materials, several antiquarians will not allow them to have belonged to the real Temple of Diana.

<small>A. A. C. 356.</small>

It is not my purpose to dispute with these learned gentlemen, I shall only observe, that none of them have made the columns of this Temple more than sixty feet high.

According

According to Palladio's meafurement of the pillars to the portico of the celebrated Rotunda at Rome, which has univerfally been accepted as a proper ftandard, the height of the Corinthian column is twenty modules.

A circumference of eighteen feet gives a module of three feet, and in common arithmetic, twenty of thefe give fixty. On thefe proportions then, the fragment I mention formed a column of the exact height handed down to us of thofe of the Temple of Diana.

But people who wifh to diminifh the confequence of the pile I am mentioning, may fay that Palladio's proportions are liable to exceptions, which I will readily admit, that I may afk, Whether it is poffible, by any proportions, to make a column lefs than fixty feet high of a bafe and capital, in addition to a
fhaft,

ſhaft, a fragment of which is forty-two feet in length?

If either of the poſitions I take up be admitted, thoſe antiquarians who will not allow this magnificent pile of ruins to have belonged to the Temple of Diana, muſt at leaſt confeſs, that theſe ſuperb fragments muſt have formed an edifice equal to it, both in ſize and grandeur.

We alſo ſaw the remains of St. John's Church, now converted into a Turkiſh Moſque. Part of the aqueduct, and many other veſtiges of the once noble city of Epheſus, are ſtill to be ſeen. But in lieu of the Bleſſed Virgin, St. Paul, St. John, Kings, Princes, and Heroes, who rendered it ſo famous, both in ſacred and profane hiſtory, its inhabitants are now reduced to a few miſerable peaſants.

We met no manner of interruption on the road, notwithſtanding this is a time when the Government, naturally weak, is obliged to ſuffer a kind of licentiouſneſs, in order to keep the rabble in good humour, and to complete the new levies.

Never was there a more popular war than the preſent. The Turks, from every part of this immenſe Empire, are preparing to join the grand army. The ſuſpicions againſt the Emperor of Germany increaſe every day; but from the zeal and ſpirit with which every Muſſulman enters into the cauſe, one is almoſt led to imagine, that the Ottomans will make a tolerable ſtand againſt the powerful enemies by which they will be attacked.

It is fortunate for the Porte, that at this criſis her Miniſters are avowedly the beſt that ever governed Turkey. The
Grand

Grand Vizir is young and vigorous, and a pupil of the celebrated Haffan, now Captain Bafhaw, or Lord High Admiral, who is juft returned from Egypt crowned with victory. He had been fent there with the fleet, and an army alfo under his command, to fubdue the rebel Beys, in which, notwithftanding the intrigues of the Ruffians, he happily fucceeded, and, by additional proofs of courage and addrefs, has added frefh laurels to his former fame.

The Vice-Admiral, who commanded at Conftantinople in his abfence, was fent to deftroy fix Ruffian men of war, which being difmafted in the ftorm that had obliged Captain Teefdale to give himfelf up to the Turks, had anchored on the coaft of the Black Sea, and feemed to promife an eafy conqueft. But, to the great difappointment of the Porte, they had time to refit and get off; and as their efcaping was faid to be owing to to want of exertion in the Turkish Vice-Admiral, he was banished immediately after his return to Constantinople, and afterwards brought back and beheaded.

The Captain Bashaw is equipping the fleet with all possible dispatch, and will sail early in the spring, with a force that will compel the Russian squadron on the Black Sea to act on the defensive, unless their fleet from the Baltic is permitted to enter the Mediterranean, and make a diversion to the southward. But as this would be entirely depriving the Porte of every prospect of opposing, with any success, the machinations of her enemies, England certainly can never permit so decisive a step to be taken in favor of the ambitious, and to us, destructive views of the two Imperial Courts.

The Reis Effendi, or Principal Secretary of State, is said to possess sufficient

abilities

abilities to fill that office in any country in Europe. The following anecdote of him, will give you an idea of his opinion of France and England. The spirited conduct of our Court during the late disturbances in Holland, reflects the greatest honor on the King and his Ministers; and it is said, that Sir Robert Ainslie, our Ambassador at the Porte, with his usual patriotic attention to the honor and interest of his country, drew up a short narrative of that important business, and delivered it to the Porte.

At an audience afterwards given to Sir Robert, the Turkish Ministry congratulated his Excellency on the distinguished success of his Court, and the Reis Effendi, I am told, made these observations, " You have acted with all " your usual courage—but with more " than your usual wisdom. You have " carried your point without bloodshed,
" and

" and have left the French to fight among
" themfelves."

The laſt ſentence occaſioned ſome ſurpriſe; but by what I learn from the French officers who are juſt arrived, a violent convulſion in France is not far diſtant, and the Reis Effendi bids fair to prove by it, his profound knowledge of the interior ſtate of that kingdom, a knowledge which Turkiſh Miniſters are not generally expected to poſſeſs, at leaſt of nations that are not their immediate neighbours.

An army of obſervation is forming on the Banks of the Danube, to watch the motions of the Germans, whoſe hoſtile declaration is hourly expected. The Baron de Herbert has given himſelf great airs in the Divan, and threatened vengeance on the Porte, for daring to attack the ally of the Emperor, his maſter. The Turks treated theſe threats
with

with the contempt such impertinence deserved; but at the same time, with great gravity and wisdom, they informed the Baron, that they were aware of the power of the Emperor, and would be sorry to see it exerted against them; but still that, trusting to the equity of Europe, they were determined to risk this unequal conflict, rather than submit to those incessant encroachments, which, by daily weakening the Porte, and increasing the power of the two Imperial Courts, must end, if unopposed, in the total subversion of the Ottoman Empire.

The Emperor seems convinced that threats will not avail, and even at this late season, daily accounts arrive of the march of his troops towards the frontiers.

Constant skirmishes are happening between the Turks and the Russians on the borders

borders of the Crimea; and since my last letter, the Porte have received information of the capture of twelve hundred Russians, and of the Island of Taman being taken by the Tartars of Kuban. The possession of this island is of great consequence to the Turks, since it forms the east side of the straits of Wosphor Zabach, which connect the Black Sea with the sea of Azof.

To balance this success, the French, and other enemies of the Porte, give out that a General Sekell, with a corps of Russians, has routed a detachment of these same Tartars, in the vicinity of Mount Caucasus. The season, however, is too far advanced for any thing decisive to be done.

In April the Grand Vizir will take the field in earnest; but in the mean while the Moscovite troops are gathering towards Turkey, on the banks of the Dneiper,

Dnieper, the Bog, and the Dniester; and if the Emperor engages the attention of the Ottoman grand army, the Russian Generals will begin the ensuing campaign with the siege of Oczakow, and the invasion of Moldavia. Prince Potemkin will direct the former, Count Romanzow the latter; and unless some other power interferes, it is not difficult to foresee, that the Imperial Courts will soon accomplish all their ambitious schemes against this brave, but unenlightened people.

LETTER XVIII.

TO CAPTAIN SMITH.

Athens, Jan. 29th, 1788.

MY DEAR FRIEND,

WE took leave of our Smyrna friends on the 19th of January, and having passed Scio, Lesbos, and Ipsera, were off Scyros on the 21st. We wished to visit this island, because it contains the tomb of Theseus, who killed the monster of Crete, and carried off the beauteous Ariadne; but the wind not permitting us to fetch it, we continued our course by Negropont, Longa, and the Promontory of Sunium. But the next morning the wind blew so strong against us, that finding it in vain to oppose it, we crossed the Sinus Sironicus, and anchored among the little iflands of Idra. The weather continued bad for three days; it drove all the wild fowl to the fhore, and afforded us excellent fhooting, which compenfated our delay.

On the 25th we again got under way, and the day after entered the Pyræus, the port of this celebrated city. What emotion muft one feel on entering the ruins of a capital, which, from a fmall village, firft formed into a regular government by Cecrops, became fo flourifhing, and fo populous a ftate, that its citizens alone, in the famous battle of Marathon, delivered all Greece from the yoke of the Perfians.

A. A. C.
1556.

Xerxes was fo little difcouraged by the misfortunes of his father, that the moment he afcended his throne, he determined to make a fecond attempt. His army

army is said to have exceeded a million of men; and the number of his fleet was in proportion to the multitude of his troops. On his entering Upper Greece, most of the states, intimidated by the immensity of his armament, submitted to the enemy.

The Peloponnesians having the advantage of inhabiting a country almost an island, and only assailable at the narrow Isthmus of Corinth, determined to defend themselves. Themistocles infused the same spirit into the Athenians, and promoted the recall of his rival, Aristides. Their allies thinking it in vain to oppose the Persians beyond the Peloponnesus, wished all their forces to retire within the Isthmus. But the Athenians, encouraged by their former victory, bravely resolved once more to become the champions of Greece, and oppose the enemy before he entered Attica.

Having brought the allies into this resolution, a detachment under Leonidas, King of Sparta, took possession of the pass of Thermopylæ, and for some time supported themselves against all the efforts of Xerxes, and his innumerable host. But a secret path being treacherously discovered to the enemy, Leonidas was surprised in the morning by seeing the Persians in possession of the heights above him.

Xerxes had now gained a decisive advantage; but the laws of Sparta not permitting its citizens to retreat, Leonidas sent back all his detachment, except three hundred, who were natives of that city. With these he devoted himself to the service of his country, and falling upon the invaders, made a prodigious slaughter among them; but fresh numbers continually supplying the place of the slain, this great and gallant Prince

A. A. C. 480.

was

was at laft overpowered, and died with his heroic affociates, in the midft of thoufands of their enemies.

In this juncture, the Athenians confulted the Oracle, and were defired to truft to their wooden walls. Themiftocles perfuaded all thofe who were capable of bearing arms to embark in the fleet; the women and children were removed; and the town, abandoned to the enemy, fell a prey to the barbarians.

The fleet was affembled in the ftraits, within the Ifland of Salamis. Xerxes, who already talked of nothing but of extirpating the Greeks, by feizing their fhips, flattered himfelf that he had now an opportunity of deftroying them all at one blow. He therefore rafhly attacked them in this narrow pafs; but he foon found the fuperiority of the Grecian Admirals, who, by the excellence

lence of their difpofition, brought a much greater number of fhips into action than the Perfians could oppofe at one time. Their van was of courfe defeated, which threw a general panick into the barbarians, and ended in a complete victory on the fide of the Greeks.

The Perfian King, who beheld the battle of Salamis from a neighbouring height, finding himfelf unable to fupport his immenfe army, after the lofs of his fleet, retreated with the utmoft precipitation. But before he quitted Greece, he gave Mardonius the command of a large detachment, to fecure part of his conquefts; but thefe being fome months afterwards entirely defeated by Paufanias and Ariftides at Platæa, and moft of the troops the King carried with him having perifhed in the retreat, the Grecians purfued him into Afia.

Athens

Athens now rose, by rapid strides, to its highest lustre. Themistocles augmented the navy, rebuilt the city, fortified the Pyræus, and joined it to the town, which is four miles distant, by a strong fortified wall. His grand object was to throw the whole power of Greece into the hands of the Athenians; but the steps by which he proposed to attain this end, were so much disapproved, that he was banished. Accused afterwards of being concerned in the conspiracy of Pausanias, the Lacedemonian Admiral, for delivering Greece into the hands of the Persians, he was obliged to fly his country; and being pursued from place to place, although innocent of the charge preferred against him, he was at last compelled to take refuge at the Court of Persia.

There he was most hospitably entertained for several years; but in the succeeding wars, the King requiring him to lead an army against the Grecians, he suffered the greatest distress in the contest between gratitude and patriotism; and neither of these virtues being able to overcome the other, he ended the conflict by putting a period to his existence. On his being banished, Aristides succeeded him in the charge of the revenues, and Cimon in the command of the forces. The glorious exploits of this young hero almost eclipsed even those of Miltiades, his father. He gained several great victories over the Persians, by sea and land, and beautified the city with the spoils of the enemy.

A. A. C. 470.

Aristides dying, Pericles succeeded him, and became the rival of Cimon, who was banished on a suspicion of favoring the Lacedemonians, but recalled five years afterwards. He settled, for a time, the differences between the rival cities, and

A. A. C. 455.

and led them once more againſt the common enemy. And having ended a war of fifty-one years, by an honorable peace with the Perſians, he died on the eve of returning to Athens. He was ſucceeded by Thucydides, his brother-in-law, but who was ſoon baniſhed by Pericles, who now exerciſed alone the ſovereign authority.

This illuſtrious patriot was equally attentive to the proſperity, and to the beauty of the city. With one hand he enriched her with the wealth of every nation, with the other he adorned her with the works of the moſt celebrated maſters. Phidias, the famous ſculptor, flouriſhed in his adminiſtration, and it is to him we are indebted for the magnificent Temple of Minerva.

But neither his refined genius, nor his political abilities, could exempt his country from the envy which proſperity
generally

generally attracts. The splendour she had attained, and the haughtiness it occasioned, drew upon her the complaints of many of the Powers of Greece, and particularly of all those within the Peloponnesus. Animated by Pericles, Athens, although averse to hostile measures, was resolved not to submit to the attacks of the Lacedemonians, but, conscious of her resources, determined to support her dignity; and thus, undaunted by superior force, she sustained herself for twenty-seven years, against the united efforts of all her enemies, in the famous Peloponnesian war.

<small>A. A. C. 431.</small>

Pericles died at the close of the fourth campaign; but the war was continued until the end of the tenth, when a truce was concluded, on terms very advantageous to Athens. But the ambition of Alcibiades, who now began to be distinguished at Athens, soon brought on a renewal a renewal of hoſtilities. He oppoſed Nicias on every occaſion, and, contrary to the advice of that excellent General, perſuaded the Athenians to ſend a conſiderable part of their forces into Sicily, himſelf embarking on that expedition: but, being ſoon recalled, he fled to Sparta, where he joined the enemy, and became the ſcourge of Attica. In the mean while, Syracuſe was reduced to great ſtraights; but, a reinforcement arriving from Peloponneſus, the Athenians were entirely defeated, and Nicias, their General, moſt inhumanly put to death.

A. A. C. 413.

This blow diſpirited the Athenians ſo much, that Alcibiades, compaſſionating their diſtreſs, returned to his duty. At firſt he was ſurpriſingly ſucceſsful; but the fleet ſuffering a defeat whilſt he was abſent on an expedition, he was deprived of the command, for having left it in unworthy hands.

The

The Athenians had soon reason to repent this act; for, notwithstanding their fleet gained a considerable advantage under Conon, it was afterwards attacked by surprise in the Hellespont, and entirely destroyed. Lysander, who gained this celebrated victory, after subduing all the maritime places in his route, arrived at Athens, and obliged her to surrender.

A. A. C. 404.

The city now suffered all the horrors of the most cruel tyranny and oppression: but the Lacedemonians, exulting in their prosperity, as the Athenians had done before, raised up a confederacy against them, by which, after ten years slavery, Athens thoroughly recovered her liberty, and regained her former consequence; and, although Thebes, under Epaminondas, seemed for a time to rival her, she maintained her superiority over the rest of Greece, until Philip of Macedon, having defeated the Grecians

A. A. C. 337.

cians in the battle of Chæronea, obliged them to nominate him Commander in Chief of their forces.

Demosthenes had long observed the steps by which this Monarch aimed at the subjection of Greece, and endeavoured, in his celebrated orations, to rouse the spirit of his countrymen; but he did not succeed until it was too late.

Philip left his authority to his son Alexander, the Conqueror, during whose absence in Persia, the Athenians attempted to regain their liberties, but were soon suppressed by his General Antipater. On the death of Alexander, Athens again revolted, and at first obtained some considerable advantages; but Antipater, being reinforced, put an end to her triumphs, and caused her principal citizens to be put to death. Demosthenes

A. A. C.
322.

mosthenes fled; but, being detected in his retreat, he poisoned himself.

From this time, Athens was almost constantly kept in subjection by one or other of the successors of Alexander, until about two hundred years before Christ, when, being attacked by Philip III. of Macedon, the Athenians complained to the Romans, who had lately concluded a peace with the King, but now again declared war against him; and being joined by several of the Greek States, Philip was soon overcome. The only use the Romans made of their conquest, was to shew their magnanimity, by restoring liberty to all the cities of Greece.

A. A. C. 196.

In the war between Rome and Antiochus, Greece was at first a principal scene of action. In this, the Romans were again successful, and confirmed their former generosity: but, at last, finding

finding the different States constantly at variance, and one or other of them ever imploring the affiftance of Rome, they put an end to their difputes, by forming them into a Roman province. They had previoufly defeated and taken Perfeus, the laft King of Macedonia; after which, it only remained to difpel the Achæan League, which had been fo famous under Philopœmen.

A. A. C. 146.

In the war between Mithridates and the Romans, the former got poffeffion of Athens; but, after a noble defence, it was retaken the year following by Sylla, who carried its library to Rome, with many of its moft valuable pieces of fculpture and painting. Attica continued to fhare the fate of the Romans, until their great Empire was divided into the Eaftern and Weftern branches. Greece then

A. A. C. 86.

then appertained to the former, and fell with it into the hands of the Turks, on the taking of Conftantinople by Mahomet II.—A. D. 1453.

LETTER XIX.

TO CAPTAIN SMITH.

Athens, February 3d, 1789.

MY DEAR FRIEND,

ATHENS still contains near ten thousand inhabitants, and has lately been enclosed by a wall, to defend it from the irruptions of the Albanians, who are ever ripe for a revolt, and have several times plundered the town. The neighbourhood abounds with olive trees, and the French have established a small factory for the culture of them. The ancient citadel is always kept in a state of defence; and, being situated on the flat surface of an unassailable rock, it is only to be subdued by famine, or a bombardment. But what most renders it an object of curiosity, is, its containing the superb Temple of Minerva, the most celebrated work of the illustrious Pericles. But, alas! of this magnificent pile, only enough is left to give us a faint idea of its former grandeur, and to make us lament the unhappy fate of so sublime an edifice. The columns which supported the south side, and part of the front, are still standing, with some elegant metopes, which represent the exploits of the different heroes of Athens, and the battle of the Amazons: but these are every year falling down, from a violent shock the remains of the temple received, about a century ago, from the Venetians, who, in bombarding the citadel, blew up a powder magazine within it.

From these ruins of fallen greatness, it is a pleasant relief to turn our eyes to the Temple of Theseus, which, being converted into a Greek church, is still perfect.

perfect. Here the sympathetic soul enjoys the generous glow of admiration, in contemplating a monument of gratitude to a departed hero, and the satisfaction of seeing, that the ravages of more than two thousand years have not been able to affect the work of a grateful people in honor of a patriotic Prince: so may we hope, that, to the last day, it will remain a living proof of the generosity of the one, and of the merit of the other.

Theseus was the great grandson of Cecrops, and, like him, corrected the wandering manner in which his people lived, and formed them into civil societies; whence he is justly called the second founder of Athens.

In the preceding narration, I took no notice of the exploits of this Prince, because they are stories we have been accustomed to hear from our cradles, and, although founded on truth, are

generally

generally classed among those of the fabulous kind. For the same reason, I passed over the death of his successor, Mnestheus, at the siege of Troy, as well the expedition for the Golden Fleece, and the other events in which Athens was concerned previous to the invasion of the Persians.

The temple is an elegant edifice, supported by a beautiful colonnade, on a similar plan to the largest at Pestum. It was erected in the administration of Cimon, who, having discovered the bones of Theseus in the island of Shyros, where he was killed by a fall from a precipice, restored them to his native city. The metopes on the front, and part of the sides, are ornamented with basso relievo, representing the battle of the Centaurs. These, you may recollect, were nothing more than the cavalry of Thessaly, where the men were so perfect in the management of their horses, that,

when

when mounted, they were suppofed to be part of the fame animal.

The eaft gateway, which was alfo erected to Thefeus, remains tolerably perfect. It was repaired by Adrian, who added an infcription, importing that Athens was now become his city; and, indeed, by his liberality, he in fome meafure made amends for the depredations the Romans committed upon her ornaments, and earned the title of one of her founders. It was this Emperor who raifed that fuperb pile the Pantheon, dedicated to all the Gods; which, by its grandeur, elegance and beauty, juftly merited that exalted title. Out of an hundred and twenty columns, each eighteen feet in circumference, only nine are ftanding. They are of the fineft marble, with very rich Corinthian capitals. Thofe of Thefeus and Minerva are Doric.

The monument vulgarly called the Lanthorn of Demofthenes, being inhabited by a French Monk, and the octagonal Temple of the Winds, by a Turkifh Dervife, are ftill entire. The former is light and elegant; the latter has nothing but its antiquity to recommend it.; for the figures which reprefent the different winds, are fo indifferently executed, that, were not their names infcribed below them, it would be impoffible to know their qualities.

Some triumphal columns, and other monuments, are ftill left in tolerable prefervation, befides a confiderable part of the Theatre of Bacchus, and many other fragments and ruins, which I am lefs particular in defcribing, becaufe we have taken exact plans of all of them.

The channel of the Ilyffus, whofe banks were formerly fo famous, is dry, even at this rainy feafon; and I have
feveral

several times walked in its bed, as well as in the olive groves where Plato delivered his lectures. I have also been as far as the plains of Marathon, to pay my oblations at the shrine of Miltiades—an interesting scene to a Soldier, and of which my military friends may expect an exact description.

THE BATTLE OF MARATHON,

MOST RESPECTFULLY INSCRIBED

TO

THE RIGHT HONORABLE

GENERAL ELIOTT,

LORD HEATHFIELD.

This celebrated field is about twelve miles in circumference, and a day's march from Athens. It is washed by the sea on the east, and surrounded by mountains on every other side, except the south-east corner, where the flat is continued a short space along the shore, and afterwards terminated by hills. The part where this slip joins the grand plain, has a large morass in its center, which extends pretty close to the hills on one side, and near the water's edge on the other.

There are two roads from the plains to Athens; the one by the morafs, the other through the town of Marathon, which lies at the foot of the hills, nearly oppofite the center of the plains.

Miltiades' army, in point of numbers, was not equal to one tenth of the Perfians; but he knew that by waiting for them under the walls of Athens, he fhould abandon the country to their ravages, and fubmit to fee them receive their convoys, and gather provifions unmolefted; and poffibly even fubject himfelf to a famine. He therefore determined, at all events, to keep from between the enemy and the capital, and wait for an opportunity of attacking them to advantage. And this Fortune foon gave him. The Perfians having reached the plains of Marathon, accompanied by their fleet, purfued the road neareft the fea. Their van had already afcended the heights, their main body filled

filled the flat beneath, and their rear was paſſing the narrow ſpace on the ſides of the moraſs. Hiſtorians tell us, that Miltiades drew his whole ſtrength into his wings, and particularly his right, leaving his center almoſt open. But as they have not been ſufficiently minute in deſcribing the ſcene of this memorable action, I could not thoroughly perceive the excellence of his diſpoſition, until I beheld the field of battle.

The moraſs ſupplied the place of troops in his center. The ſpace on the left was but narrow, conſequently his greateſt exertions were required on his right. This the General thoroughly underſtood, and at the moment the Perſians were in the ſituation I have juſt deſcribed, he ruſhed from the town of Marathon, and by his admirable diſpoſition, brought his whole force to act on the enemy's rear.

The Perſians, encumbered and confined, and ſcarce able to uſe their arms, were inſtantly thrown into confuſion, and hewn down in immenſe numbers. The main body faced about, and advanced to the aſſiſtance of the rear. The van, confident of victory from their numbers, deſcended from the heights to purſue their ſucceſs. The whole crowded together in the narrow paſſes, making a general, confuſed attempt to break into the plain: but the Athenians conſtantly out-fronting them, and the immenſe numbers of the enemy only ſerving to incommode themſelves, and to create confuſion, they were ſlain as faſt as they advanced. At length thoſe in front, unable to withſtand the terrible carnage that raged around them, attempted to fly; but being prevented from retreating by thoſe behind them, who not having ſeen the ſlaughter, ſtill puſhed forward, they precipitately threw themſelves into the moraſs.

Victory

Victory now declared for the Athenians, who, purſuing their advantage, fell with ſuch violence on the diſordered ranks of the enemy, that to eſcape their fury, their neareſt opponents were compelled to turn, and in deſpair, forced their way through their own friends. A general rout immediately enſued, and the exertions of the Athenians encreaſing with their ſucceſs, they drove the enemy headlong before them. Near thirty thouſand Perſians fell by the ſword. Numbers periſhed in the moraſs, and the reſt, in confuſion and diſmay, eſcaped to their ſhips.

Theſe, my Lord, are my ideas of the principles on which Miltiades acted, and what I have conceived to have been the plan of the battle, from ſeeing the plains on which it was fought. I am, however, aware that one of the cauſes to which I attribute the ſucceſs of the Greeks—their out-fronting the enemy—was

was a less advantage in those days, than it has become since the invention of musketry and artillery. But although the Grecians made their grand exertions by close action, yet it is to be presumed, from the hilly, irregular country in which this army was generally to act, that it was not without a considerable corps of slingers and bowmen, who, in the disposition I have given, might act to the greatest advantage upon the enemy's flank.

It is needless to say that the Persians, by forming *en potence* along the sides of the morass, might have brought as many men into action as the Greeks; they were too much confused by the sudden attack, bordering on a surprise, to execute this manœuvre, and most likely their troops with missive weapons were not in this part of their army.

The

The most plausible objection to my plan is, that had the Persians, instead of engaging and crowding themselves in the situation Miltiades attacked them, made a retreating fight, till they passed the narrow flat, and secured the heights, it was then in their power, had Miltiades persisted in the attack, completely to surround him, by making part of the troop on the heights, in front, deploy along the eminence, and then descend in his rear, whilst the rest of the army, now advantageously posted on the heights, would probably have prevented his forcing their front.

This is, doubtless, what a good General would have done. But when the Generals are equal, how can men be expected to beat ten times their number? Miltiades was in one of those situations, where inaction is as fatal as a defeat; and it was his duty to seize every opportunity, in which it was in Fortune's power

power to favor his defigns. He acted on thefe principles, and was crowned with the fuccefs his courage deferved.

At firft the Athenians thought no praifes they could beftow, equal to the merit of Miltiades; but in my letter from Paros, I mentioned the cruel perfecution he afterwards fuffered. But the death of this great man having difarmed the malice of his enemies, they foon became fenfible of their fhameful ingratitude; and as fome atonement to the manes of their departed hero, they erected a monument to his memory on the plains where he gained his glory.

Of this facred tomb, only the bafe remains. I picked up a chip of marble that had fallen from it, and was inftantly impreffed with the idea of having this honored relick fet, with a fuitable device, in fome of the metal from the Battering Ships, deftroyed before Gibraltar,

raltar, and thus to commemorate and unite the greateſt victory of Greece, with the moſt glorious achievement of Britain.

LETTER XX.

TO CAPTAIN SMITH.

Athens, February 5th, 1789.

MY DEAR FRIEND,

ON our way to Marathon, we turned a little out of the road to see a mutilated statue of a Lion, which still bears the signs of most excellent workmanship.

We have already repeatedly viewed every thing worthy notice in Athens; but as the painter has not yet finished his drawings, we shall remain here some days longer, during which we mean to make an excursion to the Islands of Salamis, Ægina, &c. But as they contain nothing worthy description, I will close this

this sketch of the history and antiquities of this interesting city, with a short account of the religion of its present inhabitants. About one-fifth of them are Turks, and the rest Greeks.

GREEK RELIGION.

St. Paul, you recollect, visited Athens, and the other states of Greece, to preach Christianity; and notwithstanding all the anathemas the Pope has denounced against the Greeks, there is, in fact, but little difference between their religion, and that of the Roman Catholics. They equally make use of the sign of the cross; worship images; pray to the saints; have confessors; and believe in transubstantiation, although they do not kneel at the elevation of the Host. If they deny the doctrine of purgatory, they admit something very like it, in praying for the souls of the dead. Their Bishops and superior clergy are never permitted to marry; but a simple priest is allowed that indulgence once in his life, though he can never take a second wife. They acknowlege the Pope to be the chief of the Patriarchs, but deny his having the power of granting indulgences; and this was his Holiness's first reason for accusing them of schism.

It is true, there is another grand point in which they dissent both from the Roman Catholics and the Protestants; I mean the article of the Holy Ghost, which they say can proceed from the Father only. There are some less essential differences, such as their using leavened bread in the consecration of the Sacrament, and mixing the bread and wine together. And they also differ in the ceremonies of baptism, marriage, and burial. In the first they give three complete immersions. The second is performed by the priest's changing the ring from the bride's to the bridegroom's finger, saying a few words, and then from the bridegroom's to the bride's. He repeats this ceremony about thirty times, without any alteration, and when he desists, it is again as often performed by each of the godfathers and godmothers. Their funerals are like those of the savages—howling and making hideous cries till the corpse is interred, and then feasting over the grave.

The Patriarch of Constantinople is the head of the Greek Church, and has under him the Patriarchs of Jerusalem, Damascus, and Alexandria. St. Polycarp is their favorite Saint. He was one of St. John's disciples, and suffered martyrdom at Smyrna, of which he was the first Archbishop.

MAHOMETAN RELIGION.

From the religion of the Greeks, I naturally turn to that of the Turks. To have a juſt idea of this, it is neceſſary that we ſhould diveſt ourſelves of every prejudice; and in arraigning the character of a man whom death has prevented from appearing in his own defence, Juſtice ever requires, that if we do not put the moſt favorable conſtruction on his actions, we ſhould, at leaſt, treat them with impartiality.

To ſpeak candidly then, Mahomet might be a religious and a moral man. His father left him in rather penurious circumſtances, but profiting to the utmoſt by the education his friends could afford him, and always preſerving a moſt unexceptionable character, he roſe to be factor of a rich widow, whom he afterwards married; and becoming, by this connection, a perſon of ſome conſequence in his country, he felt it his duty to devote himſelf to its welfare.

He saw, with the utmost concern, that the Jews and the Christians were constantly at variance, and that Idolatry was daily gaining ground. To check the progress of a practice so unworthy the human mind, and so degrading to our Divine Maker, appeared to him an object worthy his whole attention. Filled with this idea, it became the constant subject of his thoughts, and after long revolving it in his mind, he, at length, conceived it impossible to attain his end by any other method, but by that of uniting the Jews and the Christians in one religion. And this he knew could only be effected by admitting part of the tenets of both.

For this purpose, he acknowleged Adam, Noah, Abraham, and Moses, whom the Jews regarded as their chief Prophets, to whom he added our Blessed Saviour; in commemoration of whose mildnefs and beneficence, he called him the Breath of God—the moſt flattering appellation he could offer, confiſtent with the delicacy it was neceſſary to obſerve towards the Jews. Neverthelefs, a Chriſtian cannot fufficiently lament, that he was obliged to make conceſſions to a people execrated by God. But as his only object was to reſtore the divine worſhip to its original purity, he conceived that the Almighty would not be difpleafed at the means he was about to adopt fo attain ſo laudable an end.

The firſt perſon to whom he communicated his defign, was her in whom, as a good man, he was moſt intereſted, I mean his wife. She readily embraced his fentiments, and, in a ſhort time, many of their relations adopted their opinions. Neverthelefs, the Arabs in general continued obſtinate in their fuperſtition and idolatry; and as Mahomet as yet only made uſe of the gentle methods of persuasion, his proselytes increased so slowly, that he had reason to despair of success, unless he could make it be believed that he received supernatural assistance.

Thus far his conduct is irreproachable, since we may forgive his endeavouring to compound the Jewish and Christian religions, which in him, was at worst but an error in judgment. But from this moment, be began to lose sight of the delicacy and patriotic disinterestedness by which he was hitherto actuated, and we must resign him to the lash of the Christian and Jewish divines, both of whom have agreed in stigmatizing him by the epithet of " Impostor." Nevertheless a philanthropic mind will always be inclined to pity him, and to lament that a man naturally religious, with so noble an object in view, should be drawn into measures unworthy the piety of his primitive intentions.

He

He pretended, or perhaps his enthusiasm made him believe, that the Angel Gabriel had appeared to him; and, in the name of God, charged him with his mission. But still his progress was not equal to his wishes; he therefore made use of another imposture, and declared that he had been carried up to Heaven, and conversed with God. This, and some miracles he was said to have performed, gave him an unbounded sway over the minds of the people. But the persecution of the Government increasing with his success, he was several times obliged to fly from Mecca. Hitherto he had preached nothing but peace; but his fame having now spread, and gained him many proselytes in the neighbouring states, he found himself in a condition to accomplish by force, what he had in vain attempted by persuasion. Provoked at the opposition he met with, he gave out that God, irritated at the obstinacy of his enemies, had ordered him
to

to take up arms against them. He therefore raised an army, with which he beat the Koreish, or head tribe of Mecca, in the famous battle of Bedr, and gained many other victories, each of which increasing his fame and his followers, he usurped the civil and military authority, as well as the religious, and before he died, had the satisfaction of seeing himself acknowleged by many of the Eastern nations.

The Mahometans date their Hegira from the period of their Prophet's flight from Mecca to Medina, during which such miracles, they say, were performed in his favor, that it was no longer possible to doubt his being the Messenger of God.

A. D. 622.

In addition to his being an Impostor, and making use of violent measures, it is farther objected against Mahomet, that he makes his paradise consist in sensual pleasures;

pleasures; but in this he conformed to the dispositions of the people he held it out to. He tells them that it is inhabited by female angels, whose charms surpass conception, and who, although adorned by the most delicate modesty, will yield to the embraces of the Faithful. That they live in large pavilions of hollow pearls, in the midst of refreshing fountains and shady groves, abounding with the most delicious fruits. Besides which, the fleetest horses, elegantly caparisoned, and every thing else they may desire, will immediately spring up for them.

His faith consists in belief in God, and predestination; in his Angels, his Scriptures, and his Prophets; in the Resurrection and final Judgment. On that awful day the principal questions asked the Mahometans will be, How they spent their time? How they acquired and used their wealth? What use they

they made of their knowledge? and how they exercised their bodies?

Infidels and hypocrites will be damned without redemption; but the good and bad actions of the Mahometans will be balanced against each other, and the punishments of the guilty will be in proportion to their sins; the slightest of which will be nine hundred years confinement in a hell, so very hot as to make the brain boil through the skull; and the heaviest nine thousand in a place where the heat is seven times more horrible.

Oppressors, and such as have been guilty of malice or injustice, will be obliged to suffer in the next world for the sins of those whom they injured in this. An idea that cannot be too much admired.

Another

Another striking instance of the humanity of Mahomet's disposition, is the great encomiums he conferred upon Charity. He tells his followers that nothing will be more acceptable to God than alms; and to shew our gratitude to him for those we are constantly receiving at his hands, he orders that they shall pray at least five times a day; and that there may be no excuse for neglecting this duty, the muezzins are obliged to ascend the steeples at stated times, and there apprise the people that " it is time to " pray."

In this we see both gratitude and wisdom; and to do ample justice to Mahomet, it only remains to examine how far his religion tended to promote the happiness and prosperity of his brethren. To do this, we must keep their country in view. It will then readily occur to us, that the Arabians living in a state of warfare,

warfare, population must necessarily decrease, and the number of women considerably exceed that of the men. What remedy could he apply to this evil, but a plurality of wives? Or how put a stop to drunkenness, but by prohibiting wine? The climate of Arabia is hot; heat produces wantonness, wantonness leads to prostitution, and prostitution creates sin, disease, and depopulation. These are crying evils, and the only method to prevent them was, by forbidding every intercourse between the two sexes, man and wife only excepted. For she must be an abandoned woman indeed, who will make the first advances to impure love, and these to a man to whom she had never before spoken.

But as a farther encouragement to population, and that the female captives taken in war might be of service to the

the ſtate, he tolerates maſters lying with their ſlaves, who, on their part, are to preſerve all the modeſty and diſcretion of a wife, and in return, are always to be treated with tenderneſs.

That Mahomet allowed theſe indulgences, more through policy than inclination, is evident, ſince even his bittereſt enemies have never accuſed him of bigamy, or of impure love, before the death of his firſt wife. If he afterwards became abandoned, it is no wonder, for he had then caſt off his pious principles; and every wiſe perſon knows, whatever pretenders to philoſophy may ſay, that a man, when he abandons religion, generally abandons morality alſo.

Upon the whole, I believe, this is by much the moſt favorable account ever written

written of Mahomet by a Chriſtian; yet, if we analyze the writings of our own theologiſts, and ſet aſide their abuſive epithets, we ſhall find that I have ſaid nothing more than they themſelves have admitted; becauſe, not underſtanding the Turkiſh language, I have truſted to them for matters of fact, although, in juſtice to a dead man, I could not aſcribe to ambition and ſelfiſhneſs, what might originally proceed from virtue, however different a turn it might afterwards take.

To cloſe this eſſay with the candour with which I have conducted it, we muſt allow, that as a patriot and a politician, Mahomet merits a great ſhare of our commendation. But how unworthy a divine miſſion will his latter conduct appear, when compared with that of our Saviour. Neither perſecution nor torture, could provoke the Bleſſed Jeſus to a de-a deviation from his Heavenly Mildnefs; but conftantly adhering to the will of our Father, he lived, and he died for the good of mankind.

LETTER XXI.

TO CAPTAIN SMITH.

Leghorn, March 10th, 1788.

MY DEAR FRIEND,

ON the 9th of February we failed from the Pyræus, but the next morning a violent gale rising up against us, we were obliged to take shelter in our old port at Idra. During the night the wind changed, and at day-break on the 11th we again got under way, and sailing along the coast of Mycene and Argos, the kingdoms of Agamemnon and Menelaus, reached Cape Angelo at sunset; and standing to the westward, we passed between Servi and the island of Venus; and thus, for the present, took leave of the Archipelago. We saw no remains of
antiquity

antiquity on that part of Peloponnesus which we have coasted.

At day-break on the 14th, we were in sight of Mount Ætna, but the wind not permitting us to fetch Messina, we stood towards Syracuse, and in the evening tacked near the little island of Ortygia, which furnished the poets with the fable of Alpheus and Arethusa.

The next day was almost a calm, but at sunset a light breeze springing up in our favor, we entered the straits of Scylla and Charybdis, and anchored at Messina on the 16th. Here we intended to have performed our quarantine, but as it has been the custom at this place ever since the dreadful plague in 1743, not to receive vessels from any port actually infected; and a lying report being raised, that the plague was then raging in the environs of Smyrna, the Health Office

Office refused to admit us, notwithstanding our bringing a clean bill of health. We therefore put to sea the following evening, and had scarce passed Charybdis, and got out of the straits, before we were attacked by a violent storm. We were now on a lee-shore, and the darkness of the night made our situation still more unpleasant. But at the moment we were most apprehensive, the wind favored us several points. The next morning the gale abated, and in the evening the wind became quite fair; there was, however, so little of it, that we were all this and the next day in sight of the burning island of Strombolo. In the night of the 19th, the breeze freshened, and carrying us 7, 8, 9, 10, and 11 knots an hour, we saw Corsica soon after day-light on the 21st, and at five the same afternoon anchored in Leghorn roads. Lord Hervey, who has succeeded Sir Horace Mann, as Ambassador at Florence, happening

pening to be at Leghorn, interested himself in our favor; in consequence of which our quarantine was only fifteen days, and we got prattick the day before yesterday.

The town is well fortified both by sea and land, and, on account of its advantageous situation for trade, and its being a free port, it is filled with merchants of every clafs and persuasion.

Corsica being in sight of Leghorn, it forms one of the passes that intercept the trade of the Mediterranean, and is consequently an excellent station for a squadron in time of war. The road, indeed, is open, and in winter dangerous; but this evil is, in some measure, remedied by two capacious moles, deep enough for trading vessels and small frigates. And by means of a

canal

canal which communicates with the Arno, it has water carriage even beyond Florence. I shall set out for that celebrated capital, as soon as I am a little collected after the voyage.

LETTER XXII.

TO CAPTAIN SMITH.

Florence, March 23d, 1788.

MY DEAR FRIEND,

WE left Leghorn on the 18th, and, two hours after, arrived at Pisa. We remained there the rest of the day, and had just time to take a cursory view of the wonderful Leaning Tower, the celebrated Brazen Gates of the Cathedral, the Dome, the College, and the Chapel of the Knights of St. Stephen, &c. &c. Early next morning, we resumed our journey, and, at four in the afternoon, arrived at this elegant city.

From Leghorn to Florence is sixty-three miles, or, in the Italian style, eight posts,

posts, for each of which, with a pair of horses, you pay four shillings, and the driver is entitled to a fifth, which custom has increased to eighteen pence. The Italian miles being near a fourth shorter than the English, you generally go a post in an hour and a few minutes; but this depends very much upon what you give the postilions, who always take care to enquire from those they relieve. The road is good and level, and remarkably pleasant, the whole of it being in the populous and fertile vale of Arno, and almost constantly close to the river.

In the barbarous ages, after the subversion of the Roman empire, Tuscany underwent many revolutions, and remained in a state of subjection till the time of the Guelphs and Gibbelines, when the feuds of those factions, and the contests between the Pope and the Emperor, enabled the Tuscans to shake off the yoke. They were again subdued

dued by Charles V. who, having married his natural daughter to Alexander of Medicis, he gave him the Dukedom of Tuscany: but Alexander, being a tyrant, was soon assassinated, and Cosmo, son of John of Medicis set up in his place, and formally crowned Grand Duke of Tuscany by Pope Pius V.—A. D. 1570.

It is to this immortal Prince that we are indebted for the revival of the fine arts, and for the foundation of the Gallery of Florence, which each of his descendants increased and improved. The dukedom remained in their line for the space of near two centuries, when the Medicis being extinct by Duke Gaston dying without issue, it revolved to the Emperor, and is now governed by his brother.

The arts and sciences suffered no loss from this change. Peter Leopold is their most distinguished patron; and the Gallery

lery is as much indebted to him as to the moſt elegant of his predeceſſors.

Formerly, people of humble fortunes were ſecluded from the view of theſe treaſures, by the extortion of the attendants; but their ſalaries have been lately increaſed, and they are prohibited from accepting preſents, on pain of loſing their places. The pooreſt peaſant has now a right to amuſe himſelf at his leiſure in every part of the Gallery, and admittance is refuſed to nobody but ſervants. It affords matter of ſurpriſe to an Engliſhman, that valets de chambres, and footmen, who have ſo much influence every where elſe, are here excluded from places that are open to the loweſt of every other tribe.

I have not troubled myſelf about the private character of Peter Leopold; but the face of his country, the induſtry and morality of his ſubjects, and the pleaſing

ſigns

signs of an happy and increasing population, prove him a great and a good Prince. The morals of his people are one of his principal objects, in which he has so happily succeeded, that, in the general free mart of Leghorn, where formerly the trade of a harlot was as much permitted and in as high repute as any other, the houses of ill fame are reduced to a very small number; and, in a short time, prostitution will be as completely rooted out there as it already is out of every other part of Tuscany.

By a law, as uncommon as it is just, a breach of modesty is as severely punished in the male as in the female sex; and a seducer, be his rank what it will, is obliged to marry the object he has polluted. None of either sex are permitted to shut themselves up in convents; and marriage is highly encouraged. Such, indeed, is this Prince's success in promoting morality, and preventing vice among

among his people, that, different from moſt capitals, the women are innocent and healthy, as well as beautiful; and aſſaſſinations and robberies are here no longer heard of.

What a ſatisfaction will the philanthrope enjoy, when he finds that this public happineſs and virtue has been produced by the moſt laudable means. Peter Leopold thinks the lives of his ſubjects too valuable to ſacrifice even one to the gallows or the ſcaffold; but if a citizen is guilty of any tranſgreſſion, he atones for his crime by labouring on the public works, for the general good, with a label on his back, expreſſing his crime and his puniſhment.

This being the Holy Week, the Gallery will not be open for ſome days, which is no great diſappointment, ſince the fine taſte of the Medicis was not confined to their palaces only. The town

town is ornamented with many celebrated pieces of sculpture; the principal of which are, the group of Hercules rescuing Dejanira from the Centaur, by Michael Angelo; and the Rape of the Sabines, by John Bologna; a superb fountain, with Neptune in the center, drawn by four horses, surrounded by as many persons, each attended by two fawns or satyrs; a noble equestrian of Cosmo, and many other excellent statues and columns, and a triumphal arch, erected in honour of the reigning family. I should be guilty of great injustice to Peter Tacca, if I passed over his famous boar in the market-place. He forms a kind of fountain on the ground, slabbering out water in so natural a manner, that, at first, I actually took him for a hog, too lazy to remove from the wet.

The inside of the churches are neat and elegant, white and gold, with scarlet and orange curtains. St. Croix contains the

the tombs of M. Angelo, of Machiavel, and many other great men. Among a variety of paintings, two in the dome of St. John are rather singular, *Lex Scripta* and *Lex Naturæ*. The former has a forbidding look, and is muffled up like a prieftefs. The other is in all the gaiety of youth, with an inviting person almost entirely displayed.

The soft gliding Arno divides the town; but the communication is preserved by three stone bridges. The terraces along its banks are broad and well paved; and were it possible to tire where a variety of such objects as those I have mentioned are ever to be found, one has only to retire to the Botanical Gardens, or to those of the Bobile. In the former we find every plant of the medical world. In the latter we may fancy ourselves in England. They are laid out much in the manner of our pleasure grounds, with open gravel walks, and others shaded by the twining branches of the shrubs on each side; with an aviary, a green-house, seats, and summer houses. But partaking also of the Italian, it is interspersed with statues, terraces, and fountains full of gold and silver fish.

How can we sufficiently express our gratitude to those Princes who have furnished us with so many objects of innocent and laudable delight.

The elegant taste of the Tuscan Sovereigns, has been adopted by most of their Nobility, whose palaces may be considered as so many branches of the royal gallery. I have as yet only had time to visit those of Gerrini and Ricardi.

Biliberti's famous Clorinda would alone be sufficient to immortalize the former. She is asleep, relieved from the weight
of

of her armour, with nothing to conceal any part of her exquisite beauty, but one of the ribbons of her corselet, which the air has most happily directed to shelter her modesty; but which one is almost afraid will wave from her waist. In this unguarded moment, Tancred at once discovers her sex and her beauty; but notwithstanding her defenceless situation, notwithstanding her irresistible charms, and her being a chief of the enemy, there is something so invincibly sweet, so chaste, and so inchanting in her countenance, that the hero stands transfixed with love and veneration, and dares not approach her. It is impossible not to enter into all the delicacy and sensibility of his feelings, and after the first glance, I confess to you, that, like him, I dared not suffer my eyes to wander below her neck, lest hers should open and avenge my profanation. An adverse look from such an angel,

angel, would be more infupportable than the moft tormenting death.

After fo heavenly an object, one is particularly ftruck with Salvator Rofa's Prometheus, in the fame collection. He is ftretched upon his back, with his hands and feet chained down, and the vulture preying on his liver. His excruciating torments are fo forcibly expreffed, that they fill one with horror. I therefore turned away, and hurried by Dido and Æneas, by Battoni; and the Martyrdom of St. Andrew, by Carlo Dolce, and feveral other admirable paintings, to gaze once more on the divine Clorinda.

The beft pieces in the Palace Ricardi, are, the four Evangelifts, by Carlo Dolce; St. John is incomparable; a Roman Charity, and fix figures, reprefenting baffo relievo.

The houfe in which Michael Angelo lived, is ftill preferved, and his hiftory and principal works reprefented in a collection of paintings, with which the walls were hung by his fcholars. It alfo contains fome few pieces of his own, moft of them unfinifhed.

LETTER XXIII.

TO CAPTAIN SMITH.

Florence, March 26th, 1789.

MY DEAR FRIEND,

WHEN I inform you, that the Catalogue alone of the Gallery of Florence, fills a large volume, what an unconscionable request will my dear friend appear to have made, in demanding a regular description of this superb and invaluable collection.

From so young an Amateur as I am, such an attempt, methinks, would be the height of presumption—I had almost said, of profanation. But, to convince you how much I would undertake to oblige you, suffice it to say, that the part properly called the Gallery, confifts of two fides of a parallelogram of confiderable length, joined together by a third, much fhorter.

Round the cornice, the portraits of every great character, of whatever nation he belonged to, from Artaxerxes Memnon, King of Perfia, to Dr. Anthony Cocchi, who died at Florence in 1758, are ranged according to their country. Among the Englifh, I obferved Wolfey, Cranmer, Cromwell, and Monk.

The wall between the cornice and the moulding, is lined with about an hundred and thirty paintings, by the moft celebrated mafters: all are admirable; but that which particularly ftrikes me, is the Mary Magdalen from the Tufcan fchool. Her hands are joined together with an expreffion which evinces the anguifh of her foul, and the fincerity of her repentance. A fkull is on the table before her. Remorfe and Defpair, in
their

their moſt aggravated forms, are preying upon her; and yet her beauty is in all its captivating charms. Her face ſurpaſſes every conception; and the veſt, which has fallen from her ſhoulders, diſplays a neck which even an Anchorite would for ever hang upon. She herſelf, with all the earneſtneſs of her ſupplication, ſeems ſcarce to dare hope to be forgiven.—But, were there a doubt of it, ſweet Penitent! I ſhould die diſtracted.

John de St. John's Bridal Night, is another excellent painting. He has given the Bride all the fondneſs and beauty of a Venus, but has made her more than the Goddeſs, by ſhewing that the height of conjugal love, could not remove her natural modeſty.

Her handmaids are leading her into her bed-chamber; but, when ſhe diſcovers her huſband ready to receive her, modeſty overcomes her, and prevents her

her advancing. The longing Bridegroom invites her with the moſt ardent affection, and, with a ſmile of tenderneſs, ſeems amuſed with her coyneſs. She returns his ſmile, but with a kind of denial; and yet ſeems wiſhing to comply, but cannot perſuade herſelf to approach him. Her Friends are encouraging her, and the old Nurſe is growing angry at the delay. But I am preſuming to be particular. I therefore paſs over the reſt of the paintings, and come to the ſtatues and buſts, which are ranged on baſes, at regular diſtances, along the walls.

At the eaſt end, there is a Horſe, whoſe head and body excel any thing of the kind I ever beheld; but the legs are modern, and do not ſeem to belong to him.

Were only the head and neck of Leda expoſed, all mankind would allow her to be the fineſt piece of ſculpture ever produced:

duced: but, whilst we give the Sculptor every credit for his execution, we are provoked at finding him guilty of many inconsistencies.

I should not have said so much of this statue, but that you, like myself, might have been deceived by the good nature of those well-meaning, but shallow writers, who, struck with its first appearance, did not examine farther.

Ganymede is, indeed, an admirable statue; and his Eagle is much superior to Leda's Swan.

Pomona seems really walking, and with a lightness equal to the ease of her person.

As there is no superlative difficulty in forming a figure where no passion is particularly expressed, I will not dwell on Minerva, Bacchus, Apollo, Narcissus,

Narcissus, &c. &c. &c. notwithstanding the pleasure I enjoy in admiring them.

The busts contain the heads of all the Roman Emperors, and of some of their wives. The whole is closed by a famous wild boar, and the group of Laocoon.

Parallel to each of the two long sides of the Gallery, there is a set of apartments, included in what is commonly called the Gallery of Florence.

The first on the east side, contains a most admirable Ganymede, a country God, and a few more beautiful statues and basso relievos. The principal subjects of the latter, are, the Rape of Europa, and Mark Anthony's Oration on opening Cæsar's Will.

The next, called the Cabinet of Coins and Medals, contains, as well as those articles and some few busts, two basso-relievo

relievo figures of Mars and Venus, in paste exactly like porphyry; and also seven pictures, three of which are Mosaic: those of St. Peter and St. Paul are reckoned remarkably fine.

The third is called the Cabinet of Love, from a little Cupid sleeping on a table, universally allowed to be a masterpiece of sculpture. It also contains a few busts, and the walls are ornamented with twenty-seven paintings; among which is a Venus, by Titian, universally admired: but it has been observed, that she labours under a disadvantage, in being so near the incomparable one in the Tribuna.

The fourth is filled with small statues, busts and pictures.

But the room called La Tribuna is the boast of the whole Gallery. It contains the Venus of Medicis, the Wrestlers, the Listener,

Listener, and the Fawn, which surpass what I thought it possible for marble to express. Nobody that has heard of Florence, but must have read a particular description of these admirable statues: but, in obedience to your desire, I have set down the following measurements of the Venus of Medicis, taken by myself:

	Feet.	In.	10ths.
From the top of her forehead, in a right line, to the ground	4	9	7
But, as she leans considerably forward, her real height, as well as I could measure, is	5	2	0
Circumference of the largest part of her below her hips	2	11	5
Round her shoulders and her arms	3	1	3
Circumference of the smallest part of her leg	0	8	0
Of the largest	1	1	2
Of her ankle	0	8	6
Length of her foot	0	9	0
Her arms are modern, and by no means equal to the rest of the statue. Their length is	2	5	5

The paintings in the Tribuna are equal to the statues. The most famous is Titian's celebrated Venus, which justly merits the high encomiums universally conferred upon her. She is lying on a bed, with all her beauties displayed. The painter, with great judgment, has given her a passive countenance, and introduced a softness in her air, full of languishing desire, but free from lascivious wantonness. One might compare her to a most beautiful married woman, deprived for the first time of the presence of a beloved husband. In a word, nothing can be more perfect, or more delightful.

St. Catherine also by Titian, is another excellent painting, and the Virgin Mary, with the infant Jesus on her knees, like all Carlo Dolce's pictures, is divine and beautiful.

Had

Had I found the visitation of St. Elizabeth and St. John, fondling the little Jesus on the Virgin's lap, and several others, in any place but where there is so much to admire, I should have thought each of them worthy a particular description.

The next four chambers contain the Venus Anadyomene, and a few more statues in marble; together with a variety of beautiful vases, plates, cups, and tables, richly inlaid with lapis lazuli and other rich stone; near four hundred paintings in the Flemish manner; a collection of original designs, or rough sketches, of the best masters, and another of prints; but these are very inferior to those of the moderns, and are only meant to show the progress of the art.

The cabinet of jewels and precious stones, cameos, intaglios, &c. closes the Eastern range.

It

It is with great pain that I find myfelf inadequate to an entertaining defcription of thefe invaluable treafures. The picture of St. Lawrence conducted to the tyrant; Hercules after he had killed the Giants, by Alexander Allori; Helena Forman, by Paul Rubens; the pearl fifhery, in lapis lazuli, by Anthony Tempefta; the Rape of Dejanira, by Giordano; the copy of Correggio's Mary Magdalen, and many others I could gaze upon for ever. But the objects of admiration I here meet with, are too numerous to permit me to fend you even a lift of them.—I have already tranfgreffed the bounds I had propofed to myfelf; but having gone thus far, I will proceed in the fame ftyle through the apartments on the weft fide.

The firft then is called the Cabinet of Medals, and contains a well arranged collection, amounting to the aftonifhing number of upwards of fourteen thoufand.

Many

Many false antiques have been admitted, that amateurs may have an opportunity of studying the difference between them and real ones. Over the seven bureaux, in which the medals are preserved, the Labours of Hercules are represented in as many silver groupes, copied from John Bologna.

But these are not the only master-pieces contained in this chamber. Over the chimney there is a hand in relief, by Michael Angelo, equal to his most celebrated work; and the walls are ornamented by thirty-six pictures, painted at Florence.

The second and third rooms contain the portraits of several hundred painters, most of them drawn by themselves. What a satisfaction to contemplate the characters of those celebrated masters, whose works have afforded us the highest gratification. But as admittance has

never

never been refused to the most humble candidate for fame, who may choose to send his portrait, many have gained a place here, who will soon be forgotten every where else. In point of execution, my friend the Princess Belmonté, I am afraid, is among this number; but as a patroness of the arts and sciences, she is justly entitled to a place in the gallery of Florence; and, as long as St. Cecilia is held in veneration, the tuneful, the generous Belmonté will ever be remembered.

The fourth is filled with the heads of illustrious persons, and a variety of inscriptions. On one of which, Seraspandes and Rhodaspes, the sons of Phraates, are mentioned; and it is particularly valued because Justin, the only Roman historian who takes notice of these Princes being at Rome, omitted their names.

The

The fifth contains a beautiful ftatue of an hermaphrodite, which gives name to the chamber; an Adonis, by Michael Angelo; Venus Victrix; Venus Celefte, and a Bacchus. All excellent ftatues; and near fifty valuable paintings.

The prefent Grand Duke fitted up the fixth hall for the reception of Niobe, and her fourteen children, with a tafte and magnificence worthy thefe admirable ftatues.

The collection of old paintings in the next room is alfo the work of the reigning Prince. They are accompanied by feveral bufts and ftatues.

The eighth contains copies in bronze, not only of the Venus of Medicis, and the moft admired pieces in the preceding apartments, but of every other celebrated ftatue, of which the Dukes of Florence have

have not been able to procure the original. Among these are the *Quirinal* group of horses; the *Capitol* Gladiator; the *Vatican* Apollo, and Meleagre; the little *Spanish* fawn; the *Farnese* Hercules, Bull, and Flora, and many others, which the severest critics have allowed to be equal to the originals.

But it is not copies only which here ravish the sight. John Bologna's incomparable Mercury soon arrests the eye. He is absolutely flying, and in so easy, and so natural an attitude, that it is some moments before one perceives that he is supported by the breath of Zephyr, on which he is rising into the air.

From this we pass into the cabinet of bronze antiques, where a variety of miniature Gods and Goddesses, animals, and monsters; altars, tripods, and lamps; helmets,

helmets, rings, and bracelets, &c. &c. are preserved in fourteen cases.

We now close the Gallery with the Tuscan Museum, whose chief contents are the instruments used by the ancients in their funeral ceremonies, with a variety of urns, in which the burnt bones of the dead were deposited.

There let them rest in peace, and if sleep has not already overpowered you, indulge it now—I shall not be offended with you. I am aware, that however refined and extatic the satisfaction, the objects I have mentioned afford to the senses, this pleasure is not to be communicated in a description by so humble a Dilettante as your poor friend. I have, therefore, nearly confined myself to an abridgment of the catalogue, which, as I before apprised you, fills a large volume. And since a long list,
even

even of painters, and sculptors, statues, and paintings, must ever be dry and tautological, what can we expect from its epitome? But to me, I confess, it has afforded the greatest satisfaction; that of proving that to please you, I willingly risk exposing myself.

LETTER XXIV.

TO CAPTAIN SMITH.

Naples, April 23, 1788.

MY DEAR FRIEND,

WE left Florence on the 27th of March, and, on the 6th instant, sailed from Leghorn.

The little island of Elba lying in our course towards Naples, we meant to stop there, for a few hours, to examine the harbour, which, it is said, is a very convenient one for vessels watching an enemy in Leghorn Roads; but, having no wind till three o'clock in the afternoon, we did not reach it till dusk. We were now going nine knots an hour. Nothing could be seen till the morning; and,

and, as we did not think it right to lose a night's run with so favourable a wind, we were deprived of the satisfaction of informing ourselves with regard to the harbour, and of gratifying our curiosity, by seeing the natural state of the curious stones found in this island.

The wind continuing fair, we passed Mount Cercelle, and the coast of Rome, on the 7th; at day-light on the 8th, were in sight of Ischia and Capria; but, our fair wind dying away, we did not get to an anchor in the bay of Naples till the afternoon of the next day.

Mount Vesuvius is in a very different state from that in which we left it. There have been several eruptions. The sides of the crater or cone have fallen in, and the lava has given itself vent, by forcing the side of the mountain. It is now running; and, as this is a phenomenon I had not an opportunity of seeing when I was here laſt autumn, I made it my firſt object on my return.

But the violence of the eruption is over; and it has now more of the curious and beautiful, than of the awful and ſublime. The ſide of the mountain has cloſed, and the lava iſſues from it, without its ſource being ſeen, in a ſtream of liquid fire, at preſent not more than four feet wide. It moves at a flow rate, and, although ſo much a fluid as to be capable of this motion, yet it has ſuch a degree of ſolidity, that ſtones of ſome pounds weight, thrown with force, did not penetrate its ſurface. No flame was emitted by the lava, except when we threw ſticks, paper, or other combuſtible matter upon it, which immediately took fire, and blazed. Water had no effect, but that of blackening, for a moment, the part it fell upon.

After having sufficiently admired this beautiful phenomenon, we scrambled up the cone, and went into the inside of the old crater, which I find is already assuming its former state; the working of the fire in the bowels of the earth, having overcome the weight above it, and formed a chasm in its former direction, to the very summit of the mountain.

This aperture is continually widening, and will soon again become a monstrous fiery gulph. I heard several explosions below, which were accompanied by flashes of fire, which, darting from side to side, in the direction of the chasm, came up like so many immense flashes of forked lightning.

We began the ascent before sun-set; and our attention was so well engaged, that it was near day-light before we returned to Naples.

The Princefs Belmonte has renewed her civilities; and the Nobile have fent us tickets for their mufical Converfazione.

LETTER XXV.

TO CAPTAIN SMITH.

Palermo, May 2d, 1788.

MY DEAR FRIEND,

AFTER a pleasant passage of scarce forty hours, at day-break on the 26th ult. we found ourselves in sight of Palermo. Nothing can be more picturesque than this bay. It forms a large amphitheatre, with the Capital of Sicily in the center, surrounded, for some miles, by a most beautiful country, intersperfed with villas, and inclosed by romantic rocks and mountains. A calm, which lasted several hours, gave us an opportunity of admiring this beautiful scene at our leisure; and in the afternoon we anchored in the mole.

The

The town was formerly furrounded by a ftrong wall, but the fortifications are now entirely neglected, except towards the fea, where there are ftill a few weak works.

Prince Caramanico, the Viceroy, was lately Ambaffador at London. We paid our refpects to him the morning after our arrival, and he gave us a ftate dinner the next day. But we have feen nothing of him fince.

Our ftay here is rendered remarkable by the fudden death of Prince Palagonia.

Whilft other men endeavoured to reach the Temple of Fame, by making art equal nature in her moft captivating forms, this Prince ftruck out a new road, by producing fuch monfters as nature, however perverted, could never have brought forth. With him, whoever defigned signed the moſt ridiculous and unnatural object, became the greateſt artiſt. He had a number of ſculptors and ſtone-cutters conſtantly employed for upwards of thirty years, and their productions amount to near a thouſand pieces. But notwithſtanding the great encouragement he gave, and the ample field he held out, very few of his ſtatues diſplay either genius, execution, or invention. Some of them, indeed, are as extravagant as he could wiſh, but even theſe are extravagant without humour, from the total want of connection in the members. We ſometimes laugh at a body a little deformed, becauſe the parts that compoſe it may be ſet in a ridiculous point of view; but where they are totally heterogeneous, and unconnected, we may be ſurpriſed, but cannot be pleaſed. The principal pieces are birds and beaſts with human heads, and men with the heads of beaſts.

Whilſt

Whilst we were beholding this grotesque collection with a smile, half of pity, and half of contempt, I was struck by an antique bust of Cleopatra, by much the most beautiful I ever saw; but its owner set so little value upon it, that it is stuck against the outside of his house, with another of M. Anthony, nearly as good.

The dead at Palermo are never buried; but their bodies are carried to the Capuchin Convent, where, after the funeral service is performed, they are dried in a stove, heated by a composition of lime, which makes the skin adhere to the bones. They are then placed erect in niches, and fastened to the wall by the back or neck. A piece of coarse drab is thrown over the shoulders, and round the waist; and their hands are tied together, holding a piece of paper with their epitaph, which is simply their names, age, and when they died.

We of course visited this famous repository, and it is natural to suppose, that so many corpses would impress one with reverence and awe. It was near dusk when we arrived at the Convent. We passed the chapel where one of the order had just finished saying vespers, by the gloomy glimmering of a dying lamp. We were then conducted through a garden, where the yew, the cypress, and the barren orange obscured the remaining light, and where melancholy silence is only disturbed by the hollow murmuring of a feeble waterfall. All these circumstances tuned our minds for the dismal scene we were going to behold, but we had still to descend a flight of steps impervious to the sun. And there, at last, conveyed us to the dreary mansion of the dead.

But (will you believe me?) notwithstanding the chilling scene we had gone through; notwithstanding our being in the

the midſt of more than a thouſand lifeleſs bodies, neither our reſpect for the dead, or for the holy fathers who conducted us, could prevent our ſmiling. For the phyſiognomies of the deceaſed are ſo ludicrouſly mutilated, and their muſcles ſo contracted and diſtorted in the drying, that no French mimick could equal their grimaces. Moſt of the corpſes have loſt the lower part of the noſe—their necks are generally a little twiſted—their mouths drawn awry in one direction—their noſes in another—their eyes ſunk and pointed different ways—one ear perhaps turned up—the other drawn down. The friars ſoon obſerved the mirth theſe unexpected viſages occaſioned, and one of them as a kind of *memento*, pointed out to me a Captain of Cavalry, who had juſt been cut off in the pride of his youth. But three months ago he was the minion of a King—the favorite of a Princeſs—Alas! how changed! Even on earth there is

no

no diſtinction between him and the meaneſt beggar. This in a moment returned me to myſelf, and I felt, with full force, the folly of human vanity. I turned to the holy father, who gave me this leſſon. His eyes were fixed on what was once a Captain of horſe—I ſaw in them

" Read this, titled pomp, and ſhrink
" to thy original nothingneſs."

" Hie thee to my lady's chamber,
" tell her, though ſhe paint an inch
" thick, to this muſt ſhe come at laſt—
" make her laugh at that."

The relations of the deceaſed are bound to ſend two wax tapers every year, for the uſe of the Convent; in default of which the corpſe is taken down and thrown into the charnel houſe. Were it not for the number of vacancies occaſioned by the non-payment of this ſtipend, the

Capuchins

Capuchins would be unable to find niches for the number of men who muſt die every year in ſo populous a city as this.

Women are dried as well as the men, but are not expoſed. Nobles are ſhut up in cheſts.

I am juſt returned from ſeeing Prince Palagonia become a member of this ſociety. The beginning of his funeral, although ſimilar to that of every Lord in this iſland, ſtruck me as being as prepoſterous as his palace.

He was carried to the Convent in a ſedan, attended by all his houſehold. As ſoon as he entered the Chapel, the ſedan was opened, and two pages ſupported him to an armed chair. Here he was ſeated in ſtate, dreſſed in his richeſt clothes—his hair full powdered—a ſword by his ſide—his hat under his

his arm. The Nobility of the iſland were aſſembled to meet him. They all bowed to the corpſe, and after a ſhort pauſe the ceremony began.

The maſſes were interwoven in an Oratorio compoſed for the occaſion, which, notwithſtanding only two days were given to prepare it, did great credit to the compoſer; and the performers, both vocal and inſtrumental, gave him every ſupport. The exordium beginning with " Ecco il Principe preſo da " Dio." " Behold the Prince whom " God hath taken," was in the higheſt degree pathetic and affecting. The immortal Handel could not have exceeded the energy of the muſick, and the corpſe of the departed Prince carried the words with full force to the heart.

I regret that I cannot procure this excellent piece, ſince, as we are preparing to ſail on our ſecond voyage to the Archipelago, I was obliged to come on board the moment the ceremony was over.

But before I leave this place, I will raife your philanthropy, by mentioning a charitable inftitution which is here carried to a particular height. I mean a foundation, by which a number of female children are not only brought up in morality and religion, and taught fome ufeful art, that will enable them to earn their bread; but when they arrive at a certain age, and are qualified to undertake the cares of a family, portions are affigned to thofe who choofe to marry. When virgins have thefe advantages, their Guardians will never be long in fearch of unexceptionable hufbands.

LETTER XXVI.

TO CAPTAIN SMITH.

Smyrna, May 27th, 1788.

MY DEAR FRIEND,

AFTER an absence of four months, we returned here on the 24th instant, and found the Turks in the highest spirits. The Emperor has declared against them: but this was a proceeding they had been prepared for; and, far from his arms having as yet been attended with any decisive success, he tarnished them in the onset, by beginning the war in a pusillanimous style, not at all expected from so powerful an enemy.

We had scarce left this country, before advice was received of a treacherous attempt to take Belgrade; but the flovenly manner in which this enterprife was conducted, gave the Emperor an opportunity of denying his being privy to it. It proved unfuccefsful; and, as the Baron De Herbert, the Imperial Minifter, had changed his threats into negociations for fettling a peace between Turkey and Ruffia, the Porte, unwilling to provoke the Emperor to hoftilities, and in hopes that this failure would difcourage him from purfuing his defigns againft a people who were fo much better prepared than he expected, very politically feemed to admit the Internuncio's excufes for this breach of faith.

It feems, that an officer who had paffed through Belgrade, reported at Vienna, that the fortifications were in a moft ruinous ftate, and that none of the cannon were fit for fervice. On this fallacious information, orders were haftily fent to Generals Mitrowfki and Alvinzy,

Alvinzy, to pafs the Save, with a detachment of troops, who were to be supported by Generals De Gomingen and Klebeck, and to make an immediate attempt on this important fortrefs; but the latter Generals not arriving at the appointed time, and the fortifications appearing in a very different ftate from that in which they had been reprefented, Mitrowfki and Alvinzy were obliged to retreat, and to repafs the Save.

Notwithftanding the Internuncio's difavowal of the Emperor's knowledge of this attempt, accounts were foon received, that Generals Mitrowfki and De Gomingen were ordered to Vienna, to anfwer for their failure; and, on the 8th of February, Baron De Herbert delivered a formal declaration of war.

After the journey to Cherfon, the unremitting armaments which immediately followed, and, to crown the whole, the

treacherous

treacherous attempt upon Belgrade, the Imperial Manifesto, to the surprise of every body, begins in the following manner.—" All Europe have been wit-
"ness to the good faith with which the
"Court of his Imperial Majesty has,
"for many years, cultivated peace with
"the Ottoman Empire; the sincere dif-
"positions it has manifested, on every
"occasion, to preserve their good neigh-
"bourhood; its disinterested and in-
"defatigable endeavours to avoid any
"interruption of their mutual harmony,
"and its readiness to lend every office of
"mediation, to prevent any rupture be-
"tween the Porte and the neighbouring
"Courts.

"These pacific intentions, &c. &c."

Notwithstanding the serious events which this declaration must produce, it was impossible for the Porte to refrain from laughing at the bare-faced manner

in

in which the Emperor attempted to impose on the understandings of the rest of the world.

The delaration of war was read to the Imperial troops in Croatia on the 9th of February, and the same day Dresnick was attacked by them. The garrison consisted of only seventy men; but this little corps made a most gallant defence, and, small as their numbers were, they obliged the enemy to set fire to the place before they could compel them to surrender.

At the same moment a second detachment made an attempt on Sturlich, another inconsiderable post. The Turkish Commandant reserved his fire till the Austrians were near enough for every shot to take place, he then gave them a volley, which destroyed a considerable number of the enemy. The place, however, was afterwards taken; and,

and, it is said, that in revenge for the loss the Imperialists had sustained, they put all the prisoners to the sword. I cannot believe this report, notwithstanding the following account published by authority.

Vienna, Feb. 27th, 1788.

" During the attack of Dresnick, a detachment was sent to summon the Turks posted at Sturlich to surrender. They invited the Commanding Officer to advance within fifty paces on parole, when they made so brisk a fire on the detachment, as to kill fifty men, which so enraged the Imperialists, that they put the whole Turkish garrison to death."

I do not think this account at all extenuates the severity, which it admits to have been exercised; for I never knew that it was the custom to accompany a flag of truce by an armed force; neither was it very military in the German Officer to advance with his whole detachment, even had he imagined the place was going to furrender, before he fent a party to receive the poft from the enemy.

The Imperial army now took poft with their left flank on the river Korana, near Drefnick, and their right towards the mountains of Pleffivicza, fo as to have the road to Bihacz open before them.

In the mean while, a confiderable corps under Colonel Kefnowick paffed the Unna, and attacked Turkifh Dubitza, but were repulfed with a heavy lofs. The Auftrians themfelves acknowledge to have had 431 men killed and wounded.

This *coup-de-main* having failed, Prince Charles Lichtenftein was fent to commence

mence a regular siege. He took the command of the army early in March, and on the 25th of April, a practicable breach being made, the Imperialists advanced to the assault. They met a very unexpected reception, being themselves most furiously charged by the Turks, which threw them into such confusion and dismay, that they were soon repulsed, and the garrison sallying out, without giving them time to form, drove them headlong through their own trenches, burnt their works, and obliged Prince Lichtenstein to cross the Unna that very night, and secure himself on the opposite heights.

A besieged garrison routing a besieging army in so complete a style, is such an extraordinary circumstance, that I was anxious to hear what turn the Imperialists would give it. Their account is so curious a one, that I shall subjoin it for you.

Vienna,

Vienna, May 3d, 1788.

" An attempt was made by the Au-
" ſtrians on the 25th April to ſtorm
" Dubitza, but they were repulſed as
" they were entering the breach they
" had made. In return, the Turks,
" having received a reinforcement, which
" augmented the garriſon to the number
" of twelve thouſand men, ſallied out,
" and attacked the Auſtrians in their
" trenches. A general action then
" commenced, which laſted three hours,
" and though the Auſtrians were vic-
" torious, Prince Lichtenſtein thought
" proper, all his works being deſtroyed,
" to raiſe the ſiege, and on the night of
" the 25th* he croſſed the Unna, and
" encamped on the heights between
" Dubitza and Bacin, to cover the Au-
" ſtrian territories from the incurſions of
" the enemy."

* The day he attempted to ſtorm the garriſon.

Thus

Thus we see, that *though the Austrians were victorious*, their works were destroyed, the siege was raised, and their army obliged to retreat—to pass a river in the night—and to intrench themselves on the opposite heights, to defend the country of the conquerors, from the incursions of the vanquished. An odd kind of victory this.

In a subsequent account the Austrians mention Generals Klun and Schlaun being wounded, the latter mortally; and they acknowlege to have had five Lieutenant-Colonels, three Captains, four Lieutenants, and 508 rank and file killed and wounded, besides horses. Some few privates they say were missing, and two field pieces, which were advanced to the attack, were taken by the enemy.

These are the latest accounts from the banks of the Unna.

I shall

I shall now proceed eastward, and you have only to follow me in this direction along the frontiers, to have a full view of the Imperial armies in the order you will find them on the map.

While Prince Lichtenstein was laying an unsuccessful siege to Dubitza, which ended in a complete overthrow; in consequence of which we have left him on the Austrian side of the Unna, threatened in his new intrenchments, the Grand Imperial Army advanced opposite to Sabacz, on the banks of the Save, about two days march west of Belgrade, where they remained till the Emperor arrived, in order that his taking the field might be marked by a successful enterprise. But, even according to the Vienna account, Sabacz contained but 17 pieces of cannon, and the garrison amounted to only 800 men.

It

It should seem, however, as if the Austrian Generals, in compliment to their Sovereign, wished to conceal the weakness of the object of their enterprise by the pomp of the attack. A regular siege was commenced, trenches were opened, and the batteries being completed by the 23d of April, began a heavy cannonade, which soon overpowered the fire of the Turks. Nevertheless they kept possession of a few rotten walls, which served by way of outwork, till a column, composed of the riflemen of the regiment of Peterwaradin, of the free corps of Servia, and the regiment Esterhazy, advanced to storm them. On this attack the Turks retreated into the interior part of their works, and finding it in vain, in such a place, to contend any longer against the grand army of the Emperor, and a numerous train of artillery, they surrendered their post.

The Emperor gave the Turks great credit for their defence, and much to his honour, treated the prisoners with attention, sending their wives and children to their own country.

During the few hours the Austrian fire was kept up, their batteries were well served, and the troops ordered to the assault, advanced with great spirit. In short, this enterprise would have done honor to the Emperor's arms, had it been worth the time, labour, and expence he bestowed to achieve it.

His people boast, that among the trophies are twenty pair of colours, but they do not inform us how the number of standards came to be near three times that of the cannon, or why eight hundred men should have forty colours. And the Turks say, that till the Grand Vizir can find him better employment, they have no objection to his Imperial Majesty

Majesty taking every village on the Save on the same terms he paid for Sabacz.

The number of men the Austrians lost is not exactly known; the accounts from Vienna only mention that Prince Poniatowski, and the Baron de Refroy, a General of Artillery, are among the wounded.

It was supposed that as soon as the Emperor took the command of his Grand Army, that he would have besiged Belgrade, but by the latest accounts he was very quiet in the neighbourhood of Semlin.

The troops employed on the banks of the Danube, between Belgrade and Orsowa, under Generals Wartensleben and Papilla, have had several rencounters with the Turks, with various success; but the only event of any consequence,

in

in this part of the feat of war, was an attempt upon Semendria, in which the Imperialifts were repulfed with confiderable lofs.

General Fabricius, who commands the Auftrians in Tranfylvania, has done nothing decifive, and feveral of his pofts have been carried off by the enemy.

The Prince De Saxe Cobourg, a General I much admire, entered Moldavia early in March, with the moft eaftern of the Emperor's armies. This province is governed by a Greek Prince, who is appointed by the Porte, but who wifhing to give himfelf up to the Germans, fent them a fcheme to get poffeffion of his perfon, which was executed with fuch fecrecy, that in the night a detachment of the enemy carried him off from the middle of his capital.

It should seem as if the Austrians thought the possession of his person of the greatest consequence, since the moment they got him, they fled with the utmost precipitation, without attempting to destroy the magazines, or to do any other damage.

It does not, however, appear that the defection of this Chief was of any great detriment to the Turkish cause, since the Austrian General only passed through the north-west corner of the province, directing his march by Suczawa and Siret, towards Choczim, the most northern fortress in the possession of the Turks, and their chief frontier towards Poland, distant from Constantinople about five hundred miles.

The grand exertions of the Russians are against Oczakow. The Captain Bashaw sailed for the relief of that fortress on the 20th of May, but it is feared

feared that the enemy are already in possession of both sides of the Liman, by which means their ships, covered by the batteries on shore, may prevent the Turkish fleet from being of any use to the garrison.

The rendezvous of the Ottoman army was first at Adrianople, about 120 miles from the capital, and afterwards at Sophia, near two hundred miles farther on the road to Belgrade. As fast as the troops were assembled, large detachments were sent to all the garrisons on the frontiers, and there are now 80,000 men still left at Sophia; with these, and some other corps, the Grand Vizir will march against the Emperor; and should his Imperial Majesty choose to enter the Ottoman territories, or attempt to besiege Belgrade, a decisive battle must ensue.

It will be some weeks before you hear from me again from this port, since I shall set out to-morrow on a tour to Macedonia; and before I return, I propose visiting Lesbos, Tenedos, Lemnos, and several other of the Greek islands,

LETTER XXVII.

TO CAPTAIN SMITH.

Smyrna, October 20th, 1788.

MY DEAR FRIEND,

IN my last letter, we left the Austrian General, Prince of Saxe Cobourg, directing his march towards Choczim. He sat down before that fortress about the middle of March, and immediately began to invest it; but the moment the Turks were informed that the enemy had entered Moldavia, they detached a corps of 40,000 men, to drive them out of the province.

On the approach of these troops, the Prince of Saxe Cobourg was obliged to raise the siege; and, on the 16th and 17th

17th of May, he croffed the Dniefter, and retired, with his whole army, out of the Turkifh territories: but, being afterwards reinforced by a large corps of Ruffians, he again, on the 2d of July, advanced towards Choczim, and, by the 23d, the greateft part of the town was reduced to afhes. The Turks, however, continued to defend themfelves with great valour, till the end of September, when they were obliged to furrender their poft. The garrifon, confifting of about 3,000 men, marched out with the honours of war.

The grand army of the Ruffians, under Prince Potemkin; and the fleet under the Prince of Naffau, are laying clofe fiege to Oczakow. I have already mentioned the Captain Bafhaw's departure for the protection of this fortrefs. The Ruffian fleet met him at the northern part of the Black Sea; but, finding the Turkifh force much greater than

than they expected, they retreated without giving battle.

The Captain Bafhaw immediately threw out the fignal for a general chace; but, owing to the fuperior failing of the Ruffian fleet, only four of his line of battle fhips got within gunfhot of the enemy, and even thefe could keep up with them but a very fhort time.

The Ruffians made the beft of their way towards Kimbourn; and the Captain Bafhaw, the moment this partial action was over, executed two of his Captains for not having made thofe exertions he expected, and failed in purfuit of the enemy, with thefe delinquents hanging at his yard-arm.

The Turkifh fhips appear to me juft what we conceive of the Spanifh Armada; and we have feen how difficult it is for fuch a fleet to act to advantage againft an evading enemy, who, though much inferior in numbers, is considerably farther advanced in nautical skill, and in the science of artillery.

The Russians, with the utmost diligence, secured themselves within the Liman, covered by the guns of Kimbourn and the opposite batteries. The Captain Bashaw, finding their position too strong to admit of a direct attack, embarked his troops in his gun-boats and small-craft, in hopes that, by a *coup de main*, he should possess himself of the enemy's batteries, and open a passage for his ships; but in this attempt he was unsuccessful; and several of his boats, getting aground, were burnt by the enemy.

I have not heard that he has since been able to throw any succours into Oczakow; but the garrison, which is numerous and well supplied, defend themselves

themselves with great resolution; and, in a grand attack which Prince Potemkin made on the out-works, he was repulsed with very considerable loss.

The Russian fleet, though it co-operates with the army, may be said to be itself blocked up by the Captain Bashaw; and, as there is every reason to suppose that the garrison of Oczakow will be able to sustain itself till the severe weather sets in (which, in that climate, surpasses what people in England can conceive), Prince Potemkin will be obliged either to keep the field during the whole winter, to the extreme distress, and probable mortality of his army, or to risk the destruction of his fleet, which will be frozen up, and exposed to the attacks of the Oczakowians.

The following is the Imperial account of the *coup de main* attempted by the Captain Bashaw:

" Vienna,

"Vienna, July 9th.

"The Captain Bashaw, being at anchor with his fleet near Oczakow, sent all his light vessels, gun-boats, and small craft, to the number of fifty-seven sail, to attack the Russian vessels, consisting of twenty-seven sail of the same sort and size. The Prince of Nassau placed his force in a position that prevented an attack in line, and exerted himself in such a manner, as not only to repulse the Turks, but to gain a victory over them. Two of their vessels were blown up, one sunk, and the rest were thrown into confusion, and driven back, with great loss, *till they got under the protection of the Turkish ships of the line* *."

---

* This sentence is printed in *Italics*, to mark, that, though published by the Confederate and Ally of the Empress of Russia, it contradicts the account given in the Petersburgh Gazette, in which the small craft were magnified into ships of the line.

The accounts from the east of the Crimea are, that the Tartars and Ruſſians have had frequent actions, but with no very deciſive ſucceſs on either ſide.

Let us now leave the Moſcovites, and turn to the Imperialiſts on the weſtern ſide of the theatre of war.

Soon after the defeat of Prince Lichtenſtein by the garriſon of Dubitza, the Turks croſſed the Unna, in purſuit of him, and, for ſome time, preſſed him in his intrenchments; but, the moment the news of his diſaſter reached the Emperor, four ſquadrons of dragoons, and ſeven battalions of infantry, were ordered to his aſſiſtance.

To lead theſe troops, and to reanimate his army, the Emperor called forth the great Laudohn—a gallant veteran, to whom every Soldier muſt look up with
veneration

veneration and refpect. He was now in an advanced age, and had retired from the field of arms, to end his days under the fhade of his laurels. The Genius of Auftria feemed to call upon him for relief. Roufed by her cries, and by the voice of the Emperor and the People, the veteran hero regained the powers of youth, and armed once more to lead the Imperial banners to victory.

When fo great a character appears upon the ftage, we can fcarcely refrain from wifhing him fuccefs, whatever may be the merits of his caufe. An ambitious tyrant may plunge his nation into an unjuft war, and his people may be prejudiced enough to fupport him in it; but the Soldier is neither accountable for the crimes of the one, nor for the follies of the other. His duty as a loyal fubject, and his virtue as a patriotic citizen, oblige him to exert himfelf to the utmoft, whenever his fervices are called upon;

and,

and, without entering into the politics by which his country is actuated, he feels himself engaged to promote, to the full extent of his power, the success of her arms, in whatever wars she is unhappily embarked.—Such a character is Marshal Laudohn: but of his Court I by no means entertain such favorable sentiments.

As an Englishman, policy obliges me to wish success to the Turks; for I have already proved to you, that our lucrative trade to the Levant can never be carried on so much to our advantage as whilst Turkey remains in the hands of its present possessors; and, as a Philanthrope, I feel the utmost detestation of the ambitious combination entered into by the Emperor and the Empress, to extirpate the Turks, merely because Nature has been bountiful to their soil, and because their country promised an easy conquest.

These

These Powers could scarcely imagine that Europe would look on with indifference; but they trusted that they had a sufficient party to prevent any open declaration in favor of the injured Turks. These expectations, however, the disturbances in Brabant, and the total suspension of the power of France, must have frustrated. Blush, then, O Prussia! if you neglect this favorable opportunity of shewing your justice and magnanimity.—But, still more feelingly shall I say, blush, O England! if you do not, at least, insist on an honourable peace for the Turks. Let every thing the Imperial Courts may take from them, be restored; but, above all things, prevent the Russians obtaining any solid establishment on the Black Sea, or infringing the Grand Signior's right to prevent ships of force, or warlike stores, passing the Bosphorus and Dardanelles. Let the Porte, at least, sit down on the same conditions she was forced to accept by the Treaty of Cainardgie—

Cainardgie—a treaty which created her present distress—a treaty which we ourselves, in an hour of mistaken policy, compelled her to submit to, and which now, that we know our true interests, we are bound to redress.

What has become of that spirit of virtue and generosity, which, not fifty years ago, led us to enter into an expensive war, in favor of Maria Theresa, merely because she was then an unfortunate Princess, oppressed by an ambitious neighbour, whose usurpations, like those of Russia, threatened in time to affect ourselves.

It is, no doubt, a considerable abatement of the honest joy an Englishman feels in contemplating this act of magnanimity in his ancestors, to find, that ingratitude has been the only return which has been made to us. In cherishing Austria and Russia, we may really be said to have nurtured the viper in our bosom,

bosom, which, in the moment of our distress, attempted a mortal wound, by forming the *Armed Neutrality*, or, in plain language, a *combination to supply our enemies with implements for our destruction.*

If justice to the Turks, whom we have reduced to so critical a situation; if a sense of our national dignity; if our dearest interest, and commercial concerns, will not induce us to speak boldly in a moment like this, self-preservation, at least, should affect us. Let us recollect, that Russia is an evil-disposed, aspiring child; that we now have it in our power to curb her proud spirit; but that, if we neglect this opportunity, and allow her to increase in pride and in strength, in a few years, perhaps, she may trample on our breast.

Pax queritur in Bello is a favorite motto, but *Wars guarded against in peace,* is, in my opinion, a much better one; and this is the motto England ought to choose. There is nothing, in the present state of Europe, that Great Britain can in justice require, but what she must immediately gain. Let her, then, dictate terms to Russia, and check her ambitious views. If she refuses to submit, let threats and preparations to enforce them, be added; and shew me the Power who, at this moment, will dare to oppose the serious threats of England? Vengeance would soon overwhelm her.

The adverse views of France respecting the Turks, have become every day more notorious *. Monsieur *Le Roy*, a naval Engineer, who was employed in the Arsenal at Constantinople, has been recalled, and was lately here on his return

* The intrigues of the French Court have been frustrated by the Revolution in their own country.

to France. So far, indeed, have that nation carried their unfriendly meafures, that even two French Officers of Artillery, and a few Gunners, who were in the fervice of the Porte at Oczakow, have been withdrawn by the Ambaffador.

I think I have faid enough to convince you, that, both through intereft and through principle, I fincerely hope that the oppreffive views of the two Imperial Courts may be fruftrated; and yet there is fomething fo fafcinating in the appearance of a Hero, that, I confefs to you, when the accounts of his fuccefs arrived, I did not feel forry that the walls of Dubitza had not been able to tarnifh the laurels of old Laudohn.

This gallant veteran fuperfeded Prince Lichtenftein, and took the command of the army in Croatia, in the month of Auguft. He immediately advanced to Dubitza,

Dubitza, which he took on the 26th of the fame month: but he had neither to contend with the garrifon that repulfed Colonel Kefnowick, nor with the army that defeated Prince Lichtenftein; for the Grand Vizier, having refolved to invade Hungary, and to carry the war into the enemy's country, had drawn together all the troops he could collect, in order pafs the Danube in as great force as poffible; and, not thinking that the Auftrians would fo foon return to a place which had already, in this campaign, twice proved fatal to their arms, he reduced the garrifon of Dubitza to fo fmall a number, that, according to the Imperial account, at the time it furrendered, it did not amount to 400 men.

Whether it was, that the Emperor did not find himfelf fufficiently provided to carry the war with vigour into the Turkifh territories, or that the ficknefs which prevailed among his troops fruftrated fruſtrated his intended operations, I cannot pretend to ſay; but, to the ſurpriſe of every body, the grand Imperial army, commanded by the Sovereign in perſon, remained inactive in the neighbourhood of Semlin, the whole of the months of May, June and July, and a conſiderable part of Auguſt; during the greater part of which time, the Grand Vizir was not within an hundred miles of the frontiers.

This Chief was extraordinarily late in taking the field. It was not till the end of July, that he pitched his camp at Niſſa; but from this place, he purſued with vigour his grand object, to carry the war into the enemy's country.

For this purpoſe, he turned out of the direct road to Belgrade, oppoſite to which, in the vicinity of Semlin, the Imperialiſts were encamped, and, directing his march immediately towards Hungary,

croſſed

crossed the Danube, and, with his whole force, invaded that kingdom.

The Auſtrian General, Wartenſleben, who had been ordered to watch the motions of the enemy about Orſowa, occupied a ſtrong poſt in the vicinity of Meadia, from which an advanced corps of the Grand Vizir's army, drove him on the 28th of Auguſt.

According to the Turkiſh plan I ſaw of this action, the defile lies between two high mountains; and in the bottom, a little within the paſs, lies the town. The Auſtrians were encamped on the hill on the right, which was looked upon as unaſſailable on the ſide towards the Turks. But theſe enthuſiaſtic people ſtormed theſe ſtupendous heights with the moſt romantic bravery, and carried them, ſword in hand.

It was not valour only, which diſtinguiſhed the Turks on this occaſion; for the

the Serafkier who commanded, sent a confiderable detachment previous to the attack, to make a circuit, and get to the interior fide of the hill on the left, that, if his efforts were crowned with fuccefs, this corps might enable him to reap the fruit of his labours, by appearing on the flank of the enemy, and cutting off their retreat from the town. In this they completely fuccceded. Meadia fell into their hands; and General Wartenfleben was obliged to retreat towards Slatina, leaving all his magazines in the hands of the enemy.

As foon as the Emperor was informed of the invafion of Hungary, he put his grand army in motion; and, on the 30th of Auguft, he had reached Caranfebes, within two days march of General Wartenfleben's corps; but the news of this General's defeat, checked his Majefty's progrefs. On the 3d of September, however, he again refumed his march, and,

and, advancing towards Slatina, fixed his camp at Illova.

In the mean while, the Seraſkier and his detachment, after ſecuring the magazines, remained in the neighbourhood of Meadia ſome days, waiting the arrival of the Grand Vizir, who immediately advanced, to offer battle to the grand Imperial army, and, on the 10th of September, encamped in ſight of the enemy. The Emperor, however, declined the attack. The Grand Vizir, therefore, began a war of poſts, by which, in a few days, he reduced the enemy to the alternative of either quitting their poſition, or of ſeeing their retreat cut off, ſhould their intrenchments be ſtormed.

Among other movements, a conſiderable corps were ordered, on the 14th, to turn the right wing of the Auſtrians. The Turks made this attack with ſuch impetuoſity, that they completely routed all this part of the enemy's line, and the Spahis cut to pieces the whole regiment of Wurmfer Huffars.

The Grand Vizir was now enabled to cannonade the Emperor's camp; and, on the 21ſt, having brought all his ſchemes to bear, and taken every means to fruſtrate the enemy's retreat, ſhould victory crown the Ottoman arms, he advanced to attack the grand Imperial army. The Emperor, however, did not think fit to riſk the event, but broke up his camp, and retreated with the greateſt precipitation.

The Turks had now all the honour and advantages of a victory, without the trouble of fighting for one. The Emperor fled before them; and his rear, with a great part of his baggage and artillery, fell a prey to the enemy. Some thouſands of his troops were killed, or taken, and his whole army thrown into ſuch confuſion, that, in the night, two of

his

his columns, meeting unexpectedly, fired on each other.

It is said that the Emperor once attempted to rally his troops, but that, on this occasion, he himself was very near being taken prisoner.

This glorious success was announced by the guns of the Seraglio, on the 3d of October. A general Thanksgiving was immediately performed, and orders issued for proclaiming the Grand Signior *gazi*, or victorious.

LETTER

LETTER XXVIII.

TO CAPTAIN SMITH.

Conftantinople, Jan. 1ft, 1789.

MY DEAR FRIEND,

AN unexpected opportunity having offered to carry us to Conftantinople, we fet fail for the Dardanelles on the 25th Oct. having previoufly fent to defire an exprefs might meet us there, with the Grand Signior's permiffion to pafs the forts, and go up to his capital. A favor, which, through the intereft of Sir Robert Ainflie, our Ambaffador, the Porte very readily granted.

This permiffion, however, is a compliment feldom or ever paid to a man of war of any nation, except when fhe has

has an Ambaffador on board; and it was the more flattering to us, becaufe L'Iris, a French frigate, commanded by the Vifcount D'Orleans, which was lying clofe to us, applied for it in vain at the moment we gained it. To add to the compliment, the Governor of the forts which command the pafs, promifed to falute us.

Nothing could be more delightful than our voyage through thefe ftraits. The country on each fide is beautifully picturefque, and the fituation in itfelf highly interefting. The Dardanelles, you recollect, are the ancient Hellefpont, and the fpots on which the forts ftand, are famous for the loves of Hero and Leander. Behind us were the Tomb of Achilles, the Semois and Scamander, the celebrated rivers of Troy, and every point brought an interefting character to our view.

The

The day was moſt heavenly; and our ſhip, elegantly painted, and all her appointments in the higheſt order, formed in herſelf a moſt beautiful object. Every ſail was ſet, and the breeze had juſt ſtrength enough to enable her to overcome the force of the current. This occaſional ſlowneſs of her motion, added to the majeſty of her appearance, and one might almoſt have fancied that ſhe herſelf was conſcious of the compliments ſhe was receiving from the mouths of the cannon of Europe and Aſia.

The Turks at the Dardanelles always ſalute with ball, and the nearer they go to the veſſel, the greater the compliment. Each fort fired ſeventeen guns; their cannon are monſtrous, and the ſhot flying *en ricochet* along the ſmooth ſurface of the water acroſs our bows, from Europe and Aſia alternately, and throwing up the ſand on the oppoſite ſhores, while ſhouts of applauſe from the

the admiring multitude, hailed us on our returning their falute, crowned this charming morning.

It was near dufk when we got to Galipoli, where the ftraits open into the fea of Marmora, and on the 15th of November we arrived here.

The approach to Conftantinople by fea is thought fuperior to that of Naples, or Meffina, and of courfe the fineft in the world; we miffed feeing it, by entering at night—a lofs we hope to compenfate on our departure.

Travellers in general exprefs great difappointment when they get into the town; and in comparifon of European capitals, the ftreets are certainly miferable, and the buildings in general but paltry; but as they are much fuperior to any I have feen in the Turkifh dominions, I confefs

I confess that they have exceeded my expectations.

Some of the Mosques are tolerable edifices, however different from our taste in the ornamental part of architecture. To these Christians are prohibited access; but the Turks, like other people, are not always proof against bribery. I have been shewn several, and among the rest, the celebrated one of St. Sophia, supposed to have been built by Constantine the Great. But in which I was very much disappointed. The dome only is tolerable. It is supported by two tier of columns of verde antique. From this style of architecture, and the value of the marble, one would expect a rich and elegant appearance, but the magnificent effect of the double tier of columns, is lost by the entablature being supported by arches, which reduces the columns to mere piers; and thus, in comparison

comparison of other works of the ancients, the design becomes poor and inelegant. The capitals are by no means chaste, and the architecture throughout is very indifferently executed.

The Navy Hospital, though small, would do credit to any nation; and some of the Grand Signior's summer palaces, constructed in the Chinese style, display an elegant neatness which could not be surpassed, even by that ingenious people. But the Seraglio, as far as I was admitted, has nothing to boast of. I have been through most parts of the first court on the inside, which contain the Mint, and some other public offices, and have once or twice been just within the gate of the Seraglio gardens; but to the inner court no common bribe will gain a Christian admittance, except when an Ambassador has an audience of the Sultan, and this happens but once during his residence; for Foreign Ministers transact no business with the Grand Signior in person, and never visit him but on their arrival, to deliver their credentials.

We are lucky enough to be here at such a moment, for the new Venetian Ambassador is to have his audience of introduction in a few days, and has promised to take me in his suite. On this occasion, I shall have the honor of dining with the Reis Effendi, and the other Grand Officers of State, in the interior part of the Seraglio.

I have already seen the Grand Signior several times, for he goes publicly to Mosque every Friday; and I attended the Prussian Envoy when he had his audience of the Caimacan, or acting Grand Vizir, from whom I had the honor of receiving a muslin handkerchief. It is not very fine, being only intended as a mark of amity, for the Turks strictly

strictly adhere to the Oriental custom of giving presents, and their government seems to retain much of its primitive institution. Civil and religious law, as in the days of the Patriarchs, form but one code. The Coran is the book, and the Mufti the head of both. Like the practice of earlier ages, also, he who rules the state in time of peace, leads her armies in time of war. Thus the Grand Vizir is at once Prime Minister, as well as Captain-General, and Commander in Chief of the forces. The police of the town resembles the discipline of a camp; the people retire at dusk, patroles are established, and in case of fire, or any other alarm, the Grand Signior himself, and all the Great Officers are immediately abroad. Were the Sovereign to neglect appearing on occasions of this kind, it would be thought as great a reflection on him, as if, as a General, he remained in his tent when his camp was attacked.

Immense as the Ottoman Empire is, the whole number of those troops that, from being constantly embodied, can be called regulars, amount to but about twenty-six thousand foot, and a few thousand horse. Among the former are a corps of Gardeners, (Bostangi) and another of Porters (Capigi) and these are part of the Sultan's body guards. The head gardener (Bostangi Bashaw) is, by virtue of his employment, Governor of all the forts on the Bosphorus, commonly called the Canal of the Black Sea, and the first of the Black Eunuchs, is also by his Office, Governor and Commander in Chief of the Seraglio, or Grand Palace and Citadel of Constantinople.

The canal, including its windings, is about twenty miles in length, and in most parts not more than a mile wide, which defends the capital against an attack by shipping from the Black Sea, whilst whilft the Dardanelles, although an hundred miles diftant, protect it againft men of war from the Mediterranean. The laft of thefe ftraits, at the points on which the old caftles ftand, are only about 1300 yards wide; and although they expand immediately, yet for the courfe of forty miles a fhip can feldom be out of gunfhot from one or other fide.

A ftrong north wind blows all fummer, which renders it impoffible for veffels to force their way up at that feafon, and the current at all times fets fo ftrong, that even with a fair wind, they muft be expofed for feveral hours to a very hot fire. The caftles are clofe to the water's edge; they have each two tier of guns, many of the lower carry balls of eighteen inches diameter, and when an enemy is in force in the Mediterranean, the whole extent of the Dardanelles is lined with batteries.

The town properly called Conftantinople, is a kind of Peninfula, in the form of a triangle, one fide of which is wafhed by the fea of Marmora, at the north end of which it ftands; the fecond by the harbour, on which the canal opens; this fide fronts the north, and, except the Seraglio, which forms the eaft falient angle, is entirely open. There is nothing towards the fea of Marmora, except a dead wall, the Turks trufting to the defences I have already mentioned, againft an attack by fea. Neither do they feem more apprehenfive on the third, or land fide, for the ancient triple wall, which, by running acrofs from the bottom of the harbour to the fea of Marmora, cuts the town from the country, is falling to decay. I found it to be near five miles in length, and the only part of it kept in repair, is the Caftle of the Seven Towers, now converted into a ftate prifon. Englifh artillery would lay
both

both it and the Seraglio in afhes in half an hour.

Befides the triangle I have juft defcribed, the populous towns of Pera, Galata, and Tophana, which run into each other on the oppofite fide of the harbour, are alfo included in what is commonly called Conftantinople. Galata contains the dockyard and naval arfenal; Tophana the ordnance and foundry, and Pera is the refidence of the Foreign Minifters. No part of thefe three towns have even a mud wall to defend them.

The Janizaries form the chief part of the ftanding army. They are ftill highly refpected both by the court and the people, but have loft fo much of their former confequence, that at the commencement of the prefent war, the Grand Vizir broke a whole chamber, or regiment

ment of them, for shewing a spirit of discontent. A severity, which though just, none of his predecessors, nor even the Sultans themselves dared ever attempt.

Abdoul Hamet, the Grand Signior, is upwards of sixty years old; but he possesses an engaging, benevolent countenance; and I like him the more from his attention to his wives; for although he may have as many of the most beautiful women as he pleases, yet he has attached himself to one. His happy favorite is now pregnant for the fourth time, and such is the attention paid her, that the vessels in the harbour are obliged to suspend the regular method of carrying on duty, and are not permitted to fire a musket, nor to strike the bell, nor even to give the word of command in a loud voice. By which you will perceive, that the invisible chains of the fair are as powerful in Turkey as in our
blessed

blessed island; and that the rude Turk, and the generous Englishman, though different in manners, are alike sensible of the respect due to gentleness and beauty.

LETTER XXIX.

TO CAPTAIN SMITH.

Constantinople, Jan. 24th, 1789.

MY DEAR FRIEND,

THE Porte having given a decisive answer, relative to the frigates which were brought to Constantinople to be sold, we shall sail for Gibraltar immediately. We have been detained here much longer than we expected, but the hospitality and munificence of Sir Robert Ainslie, have amply compensated this delay; and it is with the greatest regret, that I see myself on the eve of leaving his society, and of quitting a place where the hearts of every one seem to wish to detain us.

Nothing

Nothing could exceed the animation of the Turks at the moment of our arrival at this capital. The King of Sweden had relieved the Porte from a great part of the force of the Ruffians, and the accounts of the glorious victories of Meadia and Caranfebes, obtained over the Emperor, were confirmed and increafed by the hundreds of prifoners who were daily brought in.

So complete a panic pervaded the Imperial troops, that on an alarm of the enemy's approach, the heavy baggage, which had been fent on towards Temefwar, was immediately abandoned, and a great part of it pillaged, and carried off by a corps of Partifans.

But at this moment, when victory, with extended wings, was following the Ottoman arms, and when each day brought them frefh advantages, the Grand Vizir fuddenly halted, and then turned

to

to the left. It was ftill hoped, however, that his operations would continue offenfive; but probably reflecting on the danger of not finding fubfiftance for fo immenfe an army, during the approaching winter, fhould he purfue the Emperor into the heart of his country, and that the Imperial armies from Tranfylvania and Moldavia might come down and cut him off from the Danube, he had determined not to lofe fight of the banks of that river; and that, inftead of purfuing the Emperor at random, wherever he chofe to lead him, he had refolved to fecure the conquefts he had made, which would enable him to winter with fafety in the enemy's country.

This opinion was, for fome time, ftrengthened by his fubfequent movements; he left a ftrong garrifon in Meadia, and his march was directed through the Bannat of Temefwar, and pointed immediately at Semlin, which, had he
taken

taken, would have secured the left flank of the chain of posts, by which it was supposed he would have inclosed the Bannat. All his motions most strongly indicated an attempt upon that fortress, and, as there was no doubt of his succeeding, the inhabitants fled with all their effects. A corps of 3000 men, who were encamped under its walls, to watch the motions of the garrison of Belgrade, retired on his approach. He had been unopposed for six weeks, and his conduct at Illova had given the Emperor so formidable an impression of his vigour and abilities, that his Majesty had gone in person as far as Arad, to put that place in a state of defence.

But now that the Grand Vizir was in sight of Semlin, instead of taking this town, and afterwards wintering in the Bannat, or in the district the Imperialists occupied in the spring, he blasted the hopes of his friends, by withdrawing his

his whole force out of the Auſtrian territories*.

I am exceedingly ſorry that I am not ſufficiently informed to produce thoſe ſatisfactory reaſons which ſo ſublime a genius, and ſo brave a man, muſt doubtleſs poſſeſs for this retrograde motion in the hour of victory. Neither can I take upon me to advance, that the ſucceſs of Marſhal Laudohn formed any part of them.

This great General having taken Dubitza on the 26th of Auguſt, marched for Novi on the 29th. The Baſhaw of Travenick retarded for ſome time his operations againſt that fortreſs, but having too courageouſly attempted to ſtorm

---

* For which he was afterwards beheaded; but as both his reſolution and abilities were unqueſtionably great, his fate was deſervedly lamented by all intelligent people.

the Austrian trenches, he was repulsed with a heavy loss. The Marshal now pursued the siege with vigour, and on the 21st of September, a practicable breach being made, he advanced to the assault, but was now in his turn repulsed, and the Vienna Gazette acknowleges, that on this occasion he lost 284 men. On the 3d of October he renewed the attack, and the garrison being by this time reduced to 600 men, were made prisoners.

From Novi Marshal Laudohn advanced to Gradiska ; but the overflowing of the Save obliged him to suspend his operations, and to retire into winter quarters.

The campaign is now closed, except in the environs of Oczakow, where the Russian fleet being froze in, the army is obliged to remain for their defence, notwithstanding that immense numbers of their men are every day carried off by the severity of the weather, and the scarcity and badness of provisions.

In the mean while the Captain Bashaw has brought his fleet here to refit, and will resume the blockade of the Russians as soon as the ice breaks. The success of this Admiral has not been so great as his force, abilities, and resolution gave the Porte reason to expect; but they are satisfied, that by engaging almost the whole attention of the Russians, he paved the way for the success of the Grand Vizir, whose victories have more than compensated in the eyes of the Turks, for the disappointment of the Captain Bashaw.

The squadron from the southward have brought in three Russian Privateers, and since there is reason to hope that
Oczakow

Oczakow * will hold out, this campaign has, upon the whole, exceeded the most sanguine expectations of the Turks. I am astonished that they have made it out so well, for their army is really little better than an animated mob under the command of a popular leader. I have searched in vain for field-days or reviews, even among the standing forces. The only thing like military exercise, that I could ever discover, was now and then two or three men firing at a mark, or practising themselves in throwing the lance on horseback.

At present the grand army is elated with victory, and formidable by the spirit infused by success; but as one or two defeats will destroy that religious confidence and enthusiastic fury, which, for a

* A magazine having blown up, and made a practicable breach, the Russians immediately advanced to the assault, and, after sacrificing four thousand men, carried the town.

time,

time, fupply the want of difcipline and fkill, the third campaign, I am afraid, will fhake this very capital, unlefs England and Pruffia forbid fuch a cataftrophe, and by refolute meafures, confirm the expectations of the Porte, and of all thofe who wifh well to the honor and intereft of the Triple Alliance.

ADVERTISEMENT.

IT was the Author's original intention to publish his work in two volumes, one of which was to contain the whole of his first voyage to the Levant, with his return to Italy, describing all the places he visited previous to his departure from Palermo, whence he set out on his second voyage to Turkey.

This voyage would have formed the second volume, but finding the time allowed him on leave of absence insufficient

sufficient to complete his design, he has been obliged, for the present, to withhold the latter part of it; and therefore, to make the first in some degree a complete work in itself, he has curtailed his journal, and added a brief account of Constantinople, and of the leading events in the present war between the Porte and the two Imperial Courts. Convinced that these would never be so interesting as at the present moment, he could not think of withholding them from the public till he should have leisure to publish his second volume. And indeed, even in the time since his letters on these important transactions were written, the scene, as he foresaw, is entirely changed, and the Russian and Austrian armies are now advancing towards Constantinople with such success, that the safety of that capital seems no longer to depend upon the Turks, but on those Powers, without whose countenance, it is to be fuppofed, the Porte would never have engaged againft fuch fuperior enemies.

The Author during his firft voyage, treated but flightly on the manners and government of the Turks. The cuftoms of thofe people being totally different from any other nation he had vifited, his refpect for the public would not permit him to offer a particular defcription on fo flight an acquaintance, efpecially as he was to return to Turkey immediately, and to pafs near a twelvemonth in that country.

He therefore defires to have himfelf confidered as being now on the point of leaving Palermo, on his return to the Archipelago; and if the indulgence of the Public fhould give him fufficient encouragement to appear before them once more, he will endeavour

vour to gratify their curiosity, by publishing the second part of his Tour as soon as his military duty will permit him.

If the Author has not been so copious as he might on Italy and Sicily, it is out of deference to Mr. Moore and Mr. Brydone, whose elegant works have been so universally read and admired, that but little can now be said on the same subject.

The very liberal and distinguished patronage with which the Author has been honored, merits his warmest acknowledgment; and he has only to add, that it now rests with the public, either to encourage him to appear before them again, or by their silence, to command his.

F I N I S.

www.ingramcontent.com/pod-product-compliance
Lightning Source LLC
Chambersburg PA
CBHW022109290426
44112CB00008B/601